No More
Baby's Mama Drama

Dear M. Sanchez—
Thanks for your support!
I hope this this book is able
to help someone in your circle.
Happy New Year!

Ayesha J. Gallion
1/2/04

No More
Baby's Mama Drama

◆

Keeping It Out of Your Life and Marriage

Ayesha J. Gallion

iUniverse, Inc.
New York Lincoln Shanghai

No More Baby's Mama Drama
Keeping It Out of Your Life and Marriage

iUniverse, Inc.

For information address:
iUniverse, Inc.
2021 Pine Lake Road, Suite 100
Lincoln, NE 68512
www.iuniverse.com

ISBN: 0-595-30305-6

Printed in the United States of America

For my Mutah

Thanks for being brave & patient enough to be my husband. May there be many more talks over tea, hearty laughs over curry chicken dinners & sweet silences in between. Imaara couldn't have been blessed with a better father, nor I a better friend. This book was completed because of your faith in me. Please know that your past has only made you a wiser and stronger man with whom I am honored to build a future.

I love you.

Contents

acknowledgements

Bina, Jacci, Lorna, Melani, Fleesie & Natashia thank you for your sisterhood, support & love. We have blazed telephone lines, written endless AOL Instant Messages & drove the Jersey Turnpike to preserve our friendships. Although there is distance between us I've always kept you right around the corner in my heart.

My siblings **Tahseena, Latifah, Waarith & Amani** for listening to me complain about any and everything.

Gershon Hinkson, my cousin/big brother, thank you for calming my nerves when I became unsure of sharing this experience and guide with others. Your last minute counseling session pushed me forward.

Dr. Fatemeh Firoz thank you for your wisdom, insight and wit. You helped me see the endless possibilities for myself as a woman, mother, stepmother and a wife. May you be rewarded for those you've inspired.

Sergeant DeLacey Davis of the East Orange Police Department thanks for being so candid and frank with me about domestic violence laws and crime in black and Hispanic communities. I appreciate you taking the time out from your busy schedule to help out a local author.

asha bandele thank you for your memoir *The Prisoner's Wife*. Through my own experience and your story I learned that we must sometimes fumble to create our own padding when life offers us a chair of thumbtacks. I, too, masqueraded in the "Easter parade on crack." Thank you for introducing me to Greg Tate.

Samira Hall since this book's inception you've been my cheerleader. You know we go way back to the days of the 34, Science High & Brandford Place. You're practically my adopted sister!

Greg Tate thank you for inspiring me to write a book PERIOD. I know that my initial ideas for writing I shared with you are far more scholastic than the subject of Baby Mama's Drama, but this was a hoop of fire I had to jump through before anything else. One day I was just fed up and I did what you told me to do. I just started writing.

Stevie Wonder, Kindred the Family Soul, Steely Dan, A Tribe Called Quest, Sting, The Sugarcubes, Patrice Rushen, Nas, Jay-Z, Meshell Ndgeocello, Earth Wind & Fire, Peter Gabriel, Bob Marley, Portishead, OutKast, Faith Evans, Garnett Silk and **The Doobie Brothers** for being the great background music that I vibed to while writing this book.

and of course

Mommy & Daddy you taught me that I didn't have to lose my grace or integrity when dealing with this planet's many misfits. Thank you for believing in my ability to maintain peace and order in my little world. I know, though, that even after 27 years, you still peek around the corners of my life with a parent's concern.

introduction

I thought that Baby Mama Drama only happened in 'hood movies and trashy commercial black fiction. I'm surprised there isn't a *Baby's Mamas Gone Wild* video out yet. I never thought that this subject would be the inspiration for my first book, far less a part of my life. But to write the first ever survival guide for wives faced with Baby's Mama Drama? It's a dirty job, but somebody had to do it.

This is not a book intended to belittle women who are single mothers. I certainly don't think that all single mothers or women who are no longer with the father of their child(ren) possess the typical "Baby's Mama" attitude. I personally know women who are no longer romantically involved with their children's father, but are energetic, wise and beautiful individuals. I admire these women as I would any other person with positive traits, but as for the Baby's Mamas of the world—I have yet to witness a significant evolution.

This is also not a book that supports men who are irresponsible, runaway fathers. Obviously there are some husbands who lead the BM on to believe that she is still a piece of candy in his personal Sweet Shoppe. If this is the kind of husband you have, then he is just as responsible for evoking Baby's Mama Drama into your life. This book was written for women whose husbands are not selfishly still in limbo about who they want to be with. I am honoring the fathers who want to remain close to their children, but are scorned by the Baby's Mama because of his decision to get married or pursue a new meaningful relationship. A good, loving father and husband is left feeling helpless and distraught because of his ex's extreme bias toward his wife. Why shouldn't such a noble and patient man be acknowledged?

Men and women need to learn the dangers of sharing their reproductive DNA with unworthy recipients so that they can reap the benefits of creating legacies from carefully planned family trees. But for many, the lesson is learned too late and by then the drama has already begun.

Purpose

No More Baby's Mama Drama is the ultimate survival guide for women who must deal with the beast and burden of their husband's past—a difficult Baby's Mama.

Here's the scenario: A woman decides to marry a man who has children from a former relationship. She assumes that her biggest challenge will be to gain the trust of her new stepchildren. Instead the optimistic bride learns that it's their mother, her husband's ex, who plans to raise hell. This vindictive offender is becoming more popularly known in some circles as the Baby's Mama (Referred to in this book as BM. BM is also an abbreviation for biological mother).

From telephone harassment to physical threats to using her children as pawns for petty redemptions, the kind of BM that this book focuses on wants nothing more than to break the spirit of her children's father and most of all, the spirit and hope of his wife.

This guide offers realistic advice for wives who are tired of being the object of BM's abuse. Women who are married to men with BMs know about the drama that can occur and frankly want the madness to stop, but the solutions have never been packaged for their convenience. The embarrassment of being associated with a BM and her drama has kept many new wives quiet for fear of hearing the familiar, "What did you expect?" or "I told you so" from her family and friends.

What is Baby's Mama Drama?

The phrase Baby's Mama Drama is derived from urban, mostly African-American society. In these cities an above average number of unmarried men and women become parents at a young age or otherwise when they are unprepared to do so. The mother, having never married her child's father, is often referred to as his "baby's mama." The father is also referred to by the mother as her "baby's daddy." These terms are used so often that they have become a part of the vernacular used in many communities and even in American humor and entertainment (movies, books, music). The title "Baby's Mama" is considered offensive by some women, who would rather prefer the title "my child's mother." I believe that the term Baby's Mama is synonymous with an ignorant state of mind that some of these mothers possess, thus my decision for the title.

The concept of Baby's Mama Drama relates to the harassment and vindictive behavior that many of these mothers inflict upon the father of their child(ren) after he has moved on to a more mature relationship resulting in marriage to a more compatible partner. Although singers, rappers and actors have portrayed

Baby's Mama Drama as an entity referred to for humor, it isn't so funny to the wives who have to deal with stalking, threats and blatant disrespect.

Baby's Mama Drama is not limited to the stereotypical streets of urban America. From homemakers to teachers to corporate managers, there are women who must deal with Baby's Mama Drama simply because they fell in love with and married a man who had children from a former relationship.

This kind of crackbrained BM is notorious for taking her jealousy, insecurity and bitterness out upon her ex-boyfriend's wife, fiancé or new girlfriend. This book does focus on the wife's point of view but many of the issues I cover are not exclusive to the wife. A girlfriend or fiancé will find that much of my advice applies to her situation as well.

My Story

Believe it or not, my husband's tenderness and grace with his children were big influences on my feelings for him. I learned to look past many stereotypical things that I heard about men and their Baby's Mamas. I welcomed his children into my life and I knew that I wanted him to be a part of my life forever.

Sounds romantic, doesn't it?

Reality will crash anybody's party, and it sashayed into mine with hair extensions and plate full of hotdogs. The Baby Mama Drama came knocking at my door even before my husband and I got married. I soon began to feel as if the sewage from the stereotypical broken and bleeding inner city family had settled in my backyard. So instead of running away from it all, I became determined to create the marriage that I knew my husband and I deserved regardless of what anyone tried to do.

In searching for books that would give me the tools to feel more empowered, I was pretty disappointed. The books that I read on blended families totally ignored what **really** happens when the worlds of Wife and Baby Mama collide. I know that the general opinion is that your husband should be the only one to deal with his Baby's Mama and that the wife should "stay out of it." But what do you do when homegirl decides that she has a few bones to pick with you? What do you do when the Baby's Mama puts you in her off-Broadway show without your permission?

What about stepchildren who are so brainwashed by their biological mother's venom that the stepmother has little chance of bonding with them? What about the wives who need to learn how to separate their dislike for BM from their treatment of their stepchildren? *No More Baby's Mama Drama* will also help the wives who feel as if their home is becoming tainted with BM's negative energy through the stepchildren.

I wrote this guide for those of you women who are still searching for real answers and not the politically correct La-La Land advice. I hope this helps.

ajg

1

so you've got baby's mama drama

❖WELCOME TO THE CLUB

If you're at the point where you've been given this book as a gift or had to buy it for yourself, take off your shoes and sit down. Your visions of that ideal blended family crumbled quickly once you realized that your marriage had the Baby's Mama Drama bug. Every time you experienced some drama at the hands of the infamous Baby's Mama **(referred to in this book as BM)** you'd be left to wonder, *How in the world did I get myself into this mess?*

Forget about those Mike Tyson Pay-Per-View fights. I'm sure that BM's fantasy would be to drag you into a boxing ring herself. She wouldn't care if her children watched on the sidelines with pom-poms and those oversized foam Number One gloves, while singing a Jaheim song off-key. *Neva G-I-V-E U-P! Go Mommy! Go Mommy!* BM's friends would have to be there, too. Since she practically melts their ears off constantly talking about you, they've been drooling like hungry dogs for a chance to see you finally get what's coming. After round one you won't be flashing that pretty little wedding ring about town anymore—unless it's in a wheelchair.

Face it. No matter what you've done to appear harmless, the woman can't stand you. Ever since the day she knew you were serious about her children's father, BM's been nothing but an overdramatic, spiteful battle-ax who's tried her best to make your life mirror that of her own reject sitcom. From telephone harassment to slander, your husband's BM just won't drop the funky attitude or behavior.

During their courtship days with their husbands, many wives recall how understanding they tried to be as to not cause friction between themselves and BM. You probably smiled, greeted her cordially and complimented her on her children. Maybe you even held a few superficial conversations with her, but somewhere along the way BM started sending some negative vibes either directly or indirectly to you.

That's okay, you told yourself. *Everyone in this situation needs time to adjust. BM must adjust to me being an influence on her children's lives. BM may not even be emotionally separated from my boyfriend. In time, she'll heal.* But you noticed that BM's attitude only got worse. By the time you married your husband, words like harassment, trespassing, fighting, arguing, restraining order and the phrase "She's crazy!" were a regular part of your vocabulary.

You also realized that your stepchildren were trained to be disrespectful toward you and sometimes even toward your husband. And although BM seemed to be giving your husband a hard time it was obvious that you were her real target. Now that you've accepted it you've also made it a point to make BM accept a few things.

You're his wife.

You're here to stay.

But the drama…oh, the drama, has *got* to go.

Here are some signs that BM has declared war against you, but remember these behaviors may be just the beginning of Baby's Mama Drama. She:

- is almost always rude to you

- never corrects her children's behavior if it has specifically offended you

- says nasty things about you to the relatives on your husband's side of the family

- has made terrorist threats toward you

- calls your home and does not use proper telephone etiquette when asking to speak with your husband

- returns or throws away clothing, books or toys that you or your husband buy for the children

- invites your husband to events concerning the children, but does not invite you

- tells your husband that you are taking him away from the children

- hates it when your husband defends you

It's pretty easy to figure out when BM is initiating a messy and unnecessary emotional war. Sadly, the children involved are exposed to her rage and are forced to take on the anger of an irrational adult. This will hurt your husband to witness, and it will boggle your mind. You may wonder, *Why would she bring about all of this emotional chaos and vengeful ignorance without taking her children into consideration? Why can't she see that she's embarrassing herself?*

Don't waste your time over-analyzing BM. Don't wish upon a star to miraculously change someone whom you probably don't even know that well. In all fairness, the BM in your life has her own story to tell. She may be clinically depressed, but unaware of her illness. She may have a problem managing her anger or grew up in an abusive home. Maybe her self-esteem is low. She could be jealous or believe that your husband should have married her instead.

Understand that your kindness, politeness or even passivity can't change the past or culture that has shaped BM into the person she is today. I don't think you have time to remold the personality of another grown woman, do you? That's what mosques, churches and mental health counselors are for. Your only job is to enjoy your life by extracting BM's drama out of it.

❖WHAT DID MY HUSBAND EVER SEE IN HER?

You probably have tried to forget many of your undesirable romantic choices from the past. Look inside of your old boyfriend file and find a guy that you thought was really cool. Remember how much fun you *thought* you had with him? Maybe you overlooked his juvenile delinquent record, his bad breath or his ridiculous Jherri-curl. Maybe he wore high water corduroy jeans or read on a 3rd grade level, even though you were both in high school. (But you thought he was fine and you were oh so happy that he was all yours.) You probably supported his future goal of becoming a rapper and stayed mums when he ditched taking the SAT.

Now imagine if you were uneducated and foolish enough to have gotten pregnant by him. In your husband's case, at the time he conceived children with BM, maybe he didn't know what the consequences truly entailed. In a weird way, you should consider yourself the lucky one.

Try to praise your husband's emotional, educational and social growth. Many times he will try to explain why or how he ended up having children with a woman like BM. Immaturity and inexperience will blur the sharpest of visions. When your husband was younger and not as wise, he probably was attracted to BM for reasons that satisfied his level of sophistication.

it was then. Your husband is not the man he was when he was with BM. Over the years your husband evolved, as most adults should. Be happy that when he grew up and became the beautiful man he is today, he was thinking clearly enough to know the difference between a rock and a ruby. And it ain't your problem that BM doesn't fit the bill for being a red, shiny ruby!

While you're wracking your brain trying to figure out what possessed your husband to tango with BM remember that beauty without common sense or dignity is worthless. Maybe BM didn't have enough strong characteristics within her personality and was willing to tolerate the person that your husband was before he did some self-searching. She's entitled to make bad judgments, too.

An old boyfriend seemingly was God's gift to you, and maybe your husband thought that a girl/woman who risked getting pregnant before planning was big fun, too. Or maybe they did plan the pregnancy, but failed to learn enough about themselves before having children. Aren't you glad that you and your husband both refined your criteria for romance?

Of course the relationship BM and your husband had wasn't a complete nightmare. Everyone has a history and a right to experience good times and bad times so that they can make better decisions in the future. You can't take that away from your husband. You had good times in past relationships, too, didn't you? Be happy that your husband was mature enough to leave behind an emotionally stagnant situation so that he could find something that he thought was better. As a happier man, he will be a better father to his children, even if he is not with the BM.

- Learning from the past is key to planning for a better future. Try to accept that your husband's involvement with BM was a bad decision, but one that gave him priceless wisdom.

- You have a past, too. Give hubby a break.

- Don't torture yourself imagining why your husband was once so attracted to BM. Today her attitude is very unattractive and ugly, and she's too backward to know that a more positive personality would grant her and her children a better life.

- There is a time and place for all things. You and your husband, the star-crossed lovers that you are, are perfect in the eyes of fate and the Creator. Focus on the present and the great future ahead.

Count your blessings and remember that it may be hard to envision your husband and BM as two people who were once emotionally and physically attached. The person who your husband was at that time may have been a man you'd prefer never to have met. He's changed for the better, even if BM refuses to.

❖NO ONE GETS A TROPHY FOR HAVING A BABY

Ever get the feeling that your husband's BM believes that since she's part of your husband's history that resulted in children, she should be awarded a gold medal or that the red carpet be spread for her entrance? No woman should boost her self-esteem through her genitalia and working ovaries. Giving birth doesn't mean the world will bow down at your feet. I certainly wasn't moved to curtsy for the BM in my husband's life. Anyone can have a baby, but just like everyone else, BM must learn that children do not make respect and reverence arrive on a silver platter at her doorstep. If she wants your respect, she must earn it.

BM has children with your husband. This means that for the sake of being a kind person and your husband's wife, you should try to treat your stepchildren with fairness and compassion. It does not mean that you must bend over backwards to befriend BM or make yourself invisible for the sake of her emotional comfort. When you see BM, if all you are moved to say is, "Hello. How are you today?" then that is certainly acceptable. No need to send in the clowns.

Some BMs become offended if the wife does not coo and drool over the children as if they were her own. In some cases, wives are still getting to know the children and are very comfortable in allowing the children their space to adapt. The wife also has the right to maintain a distant but cordial relationship with BM. No one wants to hold a phony, chatty, conversation with a BM who desperately needs a lesson in respect. By now you're probably aware that if BM notices that you or your husband are genuinely not interested in her charades or quests for attention, she will put on an even more dramatic show.

The children are here and it isn't your position to decide, hope and pray that they had never been born. BM knows that if it weren't for the birth of her children, she'd have no ties to your husband. She'd simply be his ex-girlfriend, more or less, and life would go on. Also BM knows that if she never had any children there would be no one to condone or sympathize with her outlandish behavior. There would be no admiring offspring to unconditionally love her or validate her.

If you are a wife who has decided not to have children with your husband, or if the two of you are planning a family at your own pace, BM may believe that having had children with your husband makes her better than you. She may try to smear her motherhood status all up in your face with a smirk.

There is no need to rush into having children with your husband in hopes of knocking BM off of her imaginary throne. Don't even go there! Don't turn BM's warped delusions into a baby-making contest between the two of you. Have children with your husband on your own terms and when you are both ready to become parents together. Trust me, your husband sees so much more in you than the ability to procreate. When the time is right, a planned family between a husband and a wife is one of the most beautiful experiences two people can share. Your coming-into-motherhood experience won't even compare with BM's, nor should you want it to.

If you are not nice enough, or accommodating enough for BM's self-esteem needs, she may lash out at you through your husband or even to your face. She might threaten your husband with not seeing the children, or may imply that you, the wife, does not like the children when in fact, it is her unacceptable behavior that is unattractive. Perhaps she is desperate for your approval or attention to validate her as someone important, since all she has is her children. It could be that having children is BM's only accomplishment to tote.

I clearly remember when my husband's BM insisted that I didn't like their children. The truth is that whenever I was with them and my husband, I had entertained them, cooked for them and told them wonderful stories before bed. BM knew that I had never hurt or ill-treated her children, but she also knew that I was far from impressed with her manners and behavior. I didn't kowtow to BM and she didn't like it, but that was (and still is) her problem to solve, not mine. Sorry, but I only go into a dither over seeing my husband in a new suit or Meshell Ndgeocello live in concert. I hardly lift an eyebrow for much else.

Motherhood is a privilege, not a tool to use for self-validation. Although Mother's Day is a recognized holiday, BM's children are the only people who might feel compelled to make her feel like a saint. You nor your husband have to excuse her behavior simply because she gave birth to his children. The only people that will be impressed with and indebted to BM unconditionally are her children, and even after a while they will form their own opinions of Mommie Dearest.

I came to know of BM's existence through my husband. The last time I checked there was no social rule that said I had to become over-stimulated and chipper when BM and I shared the same space. In the beginning I tried my best to smile a lot and assume a non-threatening demeanor. But in the end BM had proven herself to be a person from whom I'd rather keep my distance. By nature, I'm a cool and calm woman of few words when I choose to be. BM gave me no reason to overextend myself toward her.

And like me, your lack of reverence for BM is rooted in her behavior. Most likely your husband is just as disinterested in her as you are. BM will only perceive this as your influence on the father of her children, and will blame you for having what she believes is your negative influence on him. She fails to understand that you and your husband can enjoy the children without inviting her to the love fest.

Don't be intimidated by BM's motherhood status. Her behavior already proves that she takes the privilege for granted.

- BM's working uterus doesn't mean she deserves a trophy. Her having children with your husband shouldn't automatically grant her your respect.

- Don't rush out and try to get pregnant to prove something to BM. Your future children deserve to be born out of love, not vengeance or ignorance.

- If you do not want to become too familiar with BM, that's fine. Remain as cordial and as respectful as her behavior allows.

- BM's children are your husband's children and they are the only ones that deserve your attention.

- BM may believe that she is as important to your husband as she is to their children. She will have to find other ways to boost her ego.

- BM may resent you for your confidence in the face of a woman who has been intimate with your husband in the past. While she lives in the past, remind yourself that the only woman who deserves a trophy is the woman who has maintains her dignity and couth at all times.

❖IT'S OVER AND SHE JUST WON'T LET GO

This is one of the most annoying things about an off-balanced BM. There's nothing more disgusting than seeing some audacious chick throwing herself at your man. Relax, girl and put your earrings back on. It's probably hard for BM to get over their relationship, marriage, young love, one-night stand or whatever the circumstances were that brought them together long ago.

Think about it. BM must look into the faces of children that may be the spitting image of your husband. The children may ask constantly about him or may want to spend an increasing amount of time with him. BM's memory of your husband can sometimes cause her to get stuck in the past, with an unwilling desire to give up what will never again be.

Wives should encourage their husbands to continue being a good father to his children with BM. Ideally BM and your hubby should have a good co-parenting relationship, right? Well that only works with responsible and sane BMs. With your husband's BM most likely it's a totally different story. One reason for this is that his BM refuses to accept or respect that her children's father is married. M-A-R-R-I-E-D.

For example, your husband may attempt to speak with BM about the educational progress of his son. Some BMs are famous for veering from the topic of the child and going into an angry soliloquy about how your husband "left" them. BM may accuse him of leaving his children to be raised by her current boyfriend live-in boyfriend or temporary fiancée. **A responsible BM would be grateful that her child's father is no longer living with them if their relationship wasn't healthy. A mature BM would stick to the topic and discuss their son's educational progress.** I know, you're thinking *Why would a responsible BM want her child to witness an unhealthy relationship anyway?*

BM's emotional wounds often lead her to say things to our husbands that leave the children on the back burner. If the relationship is over, then out of respect for her children's father's marriage, **the children should be the only issue between BM and your husband**. Any relationship issues are truly irrelevant, unless, that is BM is still in denial about her romantic status with your husband. She has yet to realize that she must find closure, and that closure doesn't lie in a heated argument with your husband. That's your husband and you're the only woman (besides his mamma, grandmamma, aunts and his sisters) that should have the gall to get into a heated, impassioned argument with him. Everyone else should be wise enough to take a time out and come correct. Consequently, important issues are not resolved such as the behavior or development of their children.

Here's another example. BM may find reasons to call your husband with an attempt to gain his sympathy. She may call and complain about her job. Maybe she'll talk about some elderly relative who is sick, while seeking charity attention from your husband. Maybe she'll ask him to fix an appliance in her kitchen. *The refrigerator's acting funny, do you mind coming over to fix it the way you used to?*

Some husbands are silly enough to fall for this pathetic attempt by BM, and many wives really don't want to get in the way. A wife may think to herself *The children need a refrigerator to eat healthy and fresh foods, right? What's the harm in seeing hubby off to BM's house so that he can fix their refrigerator?* You and your husband must encourage BM's independence if you want a marriage of your own.

In my case, BM had the audacity to request that my husband come over her house to cut their son's hair before he went away to summer camp. BM had already made it clear that she had no respect for me, my husband or our marriage, so I wasn't surprised. While my husband and I balked at her insane suggestion, we were even more disgusted that BM sent their son to ask such a question. If my husband would have went to their house, saddled up in the kitchen with his clippers and talked about old times with BM his son would only be more confused about BM and his father's relationship. Furthermore it would only encourage BM to live in a fantasy world where I did not exist.

Your husband, or the man he once was, is like a worn-out teddy bear to BM. He is something familiar, something without mystery. A smart BM knows that the children must accept that their father is married and doesn't share intimate space with her anymore. A smart BM won't confuse her children or pull them into her fantasy world, so she will do her best to cope, even if it stirs up old emotions. But this book is not about smart and rational BMs, is it?

Has BM ever inappropriately touched or embraced your husband in front of you? This is an area that your husband must deal with promptly and with clarity. It is up to your husband to relay his discomfort with BM invading his personal space. It is his body, and he must make sure that BM does not overstep his boundaries. The next chapter will explain more on your husband and how he can maintain his respect for you while dealing with an irrational BM.

Some BMs will also try to win back your husband's affection by sending messages through his family members or his friends. Maybe BM vented to one of your husband's friends that she's lonely. *I really miss the children's father sometimes. I know we're not together anymore but maybe we're just not meant to be together right now. Do you think there will be another chance for us?* In BM's mind she hopes that this message will be relayed to your husband and if spite permits, to you, too! She just doesn't get the message to move on. As a wife, hearing these kinds of messages through the grapevine may really test your patience. Don't you wish you could banish her to some Third World country so that you could live your marriage and life in peace? Don't worry, you can enjoy your marriage even more than she enjoys living in the past.

Have you ever seen the clothes some BMs wear around their exes? BM may wear flashy, tight clothing or paint her face with makeup as to appear very attractive to your husband. She may cut her hair, dye it, get liposuction or even buy a new car that she can't afford all in the name of enticing a man who isn't interested. BM might even make a sexual proposition toward your husband, or maybe she did so at the time you were dating. There is no reason to walk up to her and confront her at this point. Her only motive is to break you down into an insecure tragedy while hoping to build up her self-esteem. If your husband clearly explained to her that her behavior was inappropriate and disrespectful, then you have nothing to worry about.

BM may also try to make your husband jealous with a new boyfriend. She may try to make it appear as if she, her new boyfriend and the children are one happy family. Almost as if to say, *See what you would have had if you were still with me*? Little does she know that you and your husband feel sorry for the new boyfriend, as he is unaware that he is a pawn in BM's masquerade. Most likely these new boyfriends will figure it out and the cycle of boyfriend-after-boyfriend continues with another unsuspecting man.

Some signs BM may not be emotionally separated from your husband:

- BM makes herself appear to be pathetic, teary-eyed or incapable of minute accomplishments.

- BM makes sure to appear in provocative clothing whenever she expects to see your husband.

- BM uses the children to lure your husband into her house, without you, of course.

- BM has made sexual propositions to your husband after or before you were married.

- BM has behaved inappropriately toward your husband by touching him in ways that make your husband and you uncomfortable.

- BM still has photos of your husband throughout her home.

- BM talks to your husband's friends and family endlessly about you or your husband.

You may be too exasperated to notice, but BM's behavior really does make her look pathetic. She doesn't even have enough pride to care if her friends, family or even children notice her in her desperation. In BM's world the failure of your marriage would be her life's greatest success.

2

you and your husband

❖HUBBY HAS LEARNED FROM HIS PAST

Everyone makes mistakes. Your husband may not think that his children were a mistake, but he may have said that he doesn't think of BM as the ideal mother or individual. This happens to women, too. As a result of irresponsible behavior, babies are born to parents who have yet to develop their own sense of adulthood, social norms and family life. Children end up in limbo between the worlds of two adults who wish they had never crossed paths.

To fixate yourself on the mistakes of your husband's past will certainly drain a lot of your energy. The "What ifs…" and the "Why didn't he…" questions can be endless. You have better things to do than to obsess over things that can't be changed. Your husband once had a relationship with BM and they had children. It doesn't matter if you think he was stupid for making these choices because it is done and the past is sealed.

Have you ever thought that your husband's decisions in the past helped to shape him into the positive man you have today? It's true that you could do without the Baby Mama Drama, but aside from this, your husband *has* grown spiritually, socially and emotionally. He truly is not the same person from many years ago. You aren't the same either. Just as you give yourself credit for becoming a wiser, stronger and more intelligent woman, give your husband the same props, too. When you compare his temperament to BM's, the difference is striking. One person is still a backward, negative clown (BM) and the other has used discipline and wisdom to grow (your husband).

People enter each other's lives and these meetings can have lifelong consequences, positive and negative. You and your husband decided to walk the road of life and chance together. Your husband's connection to you is the only part of his life you need to focus on now.

❖YOUR HUSBAND'S RESPONSIBILITIES TO YOU

When you have married a man, who for whatever reason has children with a toxic BM, then there will be some steps your husband must take to protect the safety and peace of your marriage and home.

Some husbands don't know how to prevent their BM from sticking her dirty hands into the marriage cookie jar. The wife becomes upset with the husband for not taking control and things begin deteriorating from within the marriage. For some BMs, discord between you and your husband is like a Saturday night at the movies. It's a source of cruel and selfish entertainment. If your husband allows BM to disrespect your marriage then you can bet she is sitting on the sidelines with a bag of popcorn watching it all unfold.

Your husband only has one wife. This means that certain parts of your husband's life are off limits to other women. BM should not have the right to call him in the middle of the night to chat about the news or to argue over money. BM should not be showing up at his job for any reason, unless it's an emergency and she wasn't able to call. BM should not know any information about your marital sex life, your finances (other than what the courts allow her to know) or anything else that should remain private between husband and wife. If your husband is allowing BM to overstep some boundaries, then you and your husband need to have a talk and set some rules.

❖SETTING THE BOUNDARIES

What do you think BM's boundaries should be? This is something that you and your husband should decide together. Do you think BM should be allowed to call your home and curse you out, yet still retain her telephone privileges? Do you think that BM should be allowed to borrow your husband's car if hers breaks down? Does BM know your husband won't take her violent threats lightly and will pursue a restraining order to protect his family? Explore some hypothetical situations with your husband and come to a conclusion on what should be tolerated. Your husband should be more than willing to respect your need for comfort and privacy in your marriage. BM's feelings in this arena are not up for consideration.

Here are some general boundaries that most marriages have when it comes to dealing with an unruly BM.

1. BM does not have the right to call your home unless she knows how to behave herself when asking to speak with your husband.

2. If BM threatens to harm any member of your family, a restraining order is pursued and a police report filed, no questions asked. The safety of your family is not a game.

3. BM needs to discuss any proposals of changed custody with your husband and YOU. It is your house and no one can just "dump" their children in it without your approval. Although they are your husband's children, too, you still have a say in the decision.

4. If BM has proven to be a disrespectful virago, especially toward you, then your husband need not worry about whose side he should take. Your husband should always be on your side.

5. Always present a united front when BM attempts to argue with, slander or threaten either one of you.

6. You and your husband should make plans for the future (where you'd like to buy a home, financial investments, career changes) based on what you both desire, and not on what BM thinks you should do.

7. If BM offends anyone in your household your husband should check her immediately. If she offends you to your face or directly, then by all means, check her yourself.

8. Your husband must know that you refuse to live a lower quality of life because of BM's behavior. If he tolerates her behavior and lets it into your marriage then you will have some serious problems ahead and very possibly divorce.

9. BM has no power to dictate that you should be excluded from her children's lives when they are with your husband. If your husband has visitation and BM doesn't like the fact that you will be around them, then that is her problem. No one should dictate that you and your husband be separated at anytime or at any place.

10. Your husband should never expect you to do things (cook, dress, decorate your home) the way that BM did. He should expect you to be refreshingly individual at all times.

These are some of the guidelines that my husband and I go by in our marriage. It's not as if we have a plaque with The BM Commandments etched in, but these are standards that we created for ourselves as we learned more about how we wanted to keep our marriage strong.

Brainstorm by yourself and think about any holes that BM has tried to slither through so that she might disrupt your household or marriage. Decide what you and your husband can do to patch up the holes. After you've thought to yourself about what needs to be done, pitch these ideas to your husband at an appropriate time. If your husband just walks in from a hectic day at work, this is not the right time to strategize against BM's nonsense. Pick a time when both of you are alert, relaxed and in a good mood to discuss these matters.

As long as you remain honest, gentle and fair your husband should have no problem with setting some boundaries when it concerns BM. You may not see results or figure out what to do overnight, but in the end your marriage and friendship will be of better quality and strength.

❖UNDERSTANDING YOUR HUSBAND'S NEED TO BE A FATHER

It's true that many men have problems with the BMs in their lives because she doesn't respect his role as a father and disciplinarian of their children. As your husband's wife, friend and partner, you should be the last person to pretend that his children don't exist simply because they live with BM or BM hasn't cooperated with the court's visitation order. Your husband is a father. Give him the consideration and respect that a good father deserves, even if BM doesn't.

Allow your husband to freely interact with and enjoy his children as often as possible. It doesn't mean that he is siding with BM's negative behavior if he is kind, gentle and caring with his and BM's children. It means that he is only showing his children the love that all children should receive from a parent. This is your husband's duty as a father and also a need he has within himself. Just as a mother has the need to cuddle and be close to her babies, a father has the need to connect with his children in his own way.

I know that it's hard to be supportive in your husband's parenting experiences when BM is always trying to pit your stepchildren against you. It's so easy to withdraw totally from socializing with your husband and his children during visitation or other events that bring them together. If your stepchildren have been cruel or mean to you, then maybe you believe that your husband should be as disgusted with his children as you are. Maybe you think that his children don't and will never have the capacity to fully appreciate your husband. These are not abnormal feelings, but you must learn to stop these thoughts when you begin to feel them growing in your mind. Here are some questions that will help you.

- Does your husband enjoy being a father?

- Is he a good, kind and loving father toward his children?

- Do all children deserve to be loved and connected with both of their parents?

- Do you really love your husband?

If you answered yes to all of these questions (and you should have) then you are on your way to being an even better wife and friend to your husband. Don't block his chances to make beautiful memories with his children. It's bad enough that the BM in your life has probably told her children that you have "stolen" their father. Maybe you do want your husband to yourself sometimes, and that's nothing to be ashamed of. Many women who adore their husbands want to spend a lot of time together without interruption.

Ask your husband how he thinks you can be a better stepmother. Tell him that you're open to suggestions on how to become more supportive of his role as a father. Sometimes wives can get so caught up in how disgusting BM is that she may forget how much her stepchildren mean to her husband. It's no news that some stepmothers just aren't close or connected to their stepchildren for a variety of reasons, but you'll just make your life miserable if you tamper with their relationship to their biological father. Let your husband do all he can within reason to show his children that he will always be their father no matter what.

In the meantime, you're thinking, *Well I'm his wife no matter what. Am I supposed to just stand here while he plays Super Dad?* Of course not! Make sure that while your husband is being a wonderful dad with his children that you both have private time, too. Your husband will enjoy fatherhood and marriage if he learns how to ration his love and attention in the right places at the right times. It is your job to help your husband understand when you want his attention and how you want his attention—but it shouldn't be 24 hours a day.

❖You Don't Have to Hide Your Love in Front of Anyone

When you and your husband began dating there were probably a few people in your husband's family, including his children with BM, who squirmed at the sight of you and hubby showing affection toward each other. Maybe you rolled your eyes, rebelled and ignored their discomfort. Or like some other wives, you toned down the handholding when they were around. Now that you're married, however, you definitely don't have to pretend that you and your husband are platonic friends.

People who are still getting used to the idea that your husband is married to you will benefit from seeing you and your husband be affectionate toward one another. If you are too shy to hug your husband in front of his extended family, his children or even BM, it only instills the idea in their minds that your husband has not moved on yet. Don't be afraid that some people will feel uncomfortable in the midst of your happiness and love. If anyone doesn't like the fact that your husband is with you, or they wish he had married BM instead then that is their issue to come to grips with—not yours.

It's okay if your stepchildren see you kiss your husband good morning or if they see you sit on his lap. These are normal behaviors of loving husbands and wives. Why should you pretend to be a dysfunctional and frigid couple so that everyone else outside of your union can be at ease? Doing so would be a disservice to your marriage and to yourself.

Act like a married couple if you want others to get acclimated to your status as a wife. Don't act like a couple of young, high school students who are sneaking around behind your parents' backs. Rest your head on your husband's shoulder in the grocery checkout line. Don't clam up when your husband calls you "honey," "sugar" or "beautiful" in public. If you both love each other, there's no shame in showing this to each other. Now I'm not advocating that you fondle or grope each other inappropriately in order to ruffle the feathers of people who don't respect your marriage. I'm just telling you to be yourselves. Enjoy your life together without allowing envy and condescending behavior from outsiders to ruin your fun.

The more you and your husband become comfortable with expressing your affection in tense atmospheres, the stronger you'll become against people who would like to see your marriage weaken. This is your husband. **You** help him through his difficulties. **You** are his match for his life on this earth. No one ever has the right to make you feel as if you haven't earned the right to be or to act like his wife.

❖WHEN THE GOING GETS ROUGH, COUNSELING MIGHT HELP

There is no perfect marriage. Most new couples have all kinds of issues during the first couple of years of marriage. If it wasn't Baby Mama Drama, then it might have been something else. Sometimes, however, the discord between you and your husband may make you feel as if you just can't take it anymore. You wanna just book a flight to Martinique so that you can get as far as you can from the BM, the stepchildren and what may seem like a knuckle-headed husband.

If you and your husband have been at odds over subjects like child support, your stepchildren, BM or anything else relative to these issues then you may need help in sorting them out. For some couples arguing about such sensitive topics brings out the worst in each other. While you are trying to be your own advocate, your husband may think that you're ignoring his point of view. Or on the flip-side, your husband may try to convince you of a point he strongly believes in while you appear to be callous and insensitive. It's an argumentative cycle that can creep into the most innocent of conversations if you aren't aware of it.

When things get so bad that you're starting to question if you've married the right man, you and your husband may want to consider seeking help from a licensed therapist that specializes in family, marriage and blended family issues. If you are uncomfortable with reaching out to a therapist then you can always try reading some of the suggested books listed in Appendix B of this book. Also if there is a spiritual or religious community leader that you trust, try making an appointment for a counseling session. Whatever you choose to do, you and your husband should go beyond the limits of your marriage for help.

You and your husband can decide to get individual or couple counseling. For some women individual counseling is a great way to release the feelings and thoughts that they don't feel comfortable sharing with their husbands. For instance, if you have some really nasty things to say about your stepchildren or your mother-in-law then a therapist is the perfect person to confide in. Not only will you take a great weight off of your shoulders, your therapist will try to help you understand the root of your negative feelings so that you can ascend to a more positive place.

You can avoid hurting your husband by talking out your feelings with a neutral party, and that's just what a therapist will be for you. A neutral party **does not** mean your mother, a homegirl or your siblings. If you choose to tell people that are close to you about your problems then that's fine if they don't add fuel to the fire. But it will be very hard for your friends and family to remain objective in the advice that they give to you. A good therapist is willing to tell you when you are right as well as when you are wrong.

Now if you and your husband agree on getting counseling as a couple then that's a good thing, too. At first you both may be a bit more reserved in saying how you really feel about certain things. But it's your therapist's job to help you through this tense phase so that you can uncover the layers of what is really bringing down your marriage. It won't be an emotional breeze in the beginning but the results will be worth the initial discomfort.

What if you've already reached out to a therapist for individual or couple counseling and you think that your counselor isn't doing a good job? All counselors, psychiatrists, psychologists and therapists are not created equal. When you leave the therapist's office you should feel as if you have purged yourself. You should feel refreshed and mentally prepared to deal with the challenges that brought you to seek help in the first place. If you feel as if you are even more depressed, frustrated and in despair then something is wrong with your therapist's techniques. You and your husband shouldn't be afraid to end the sessions and find a better counselor.

Use the following checklist when assessing prospective counselors.

Signs of a good counselor. He or she:

- seems genuinely compassionate and values you as a person.
- challenges you when you are off base, even if you get angry or defensive in response.
- gives feedback and suggestions about your life decisions that seem realistic and reasonable, neither too timid nor too risky.
- is willing to help you and also educate themselves about your problems, but does not pretend that they know exactly how you feel.
- treats you as an equal and does not treat you as though you are sick and unstable.
- will not get upset is you disagree with what they have said, but instead encourages you to express yourself when you do not agree.
- believes what you tell them, never minimizes your experiences and always respects your feelings.
- does not spend time talking about their problems. Those sessions are for you, not your therapist.
- helps teach you new and healthier ways to cope.
- will never make you feel like a failure or cause you to believe they are disappointed in you if you have a slip or a relapse.
- does not act or come across as too "professional." One that is informal and casual will make you feel more comfortable.

Signs your counselor is not worthy of your time and money. He or she:

- opens up the floodgates of emotional stress without providing some means of assisting you in creating containment until your next session.
- doesn't address the problem.
- believes that childhood abuse, or living with alcohol or drug addictions (yours or someone else's) are not significant issues that need addressing.
- makes inappropriate comments to you.
- encourages romantic feelings between the two of you.
- disparages your sense of duty towards others
- in any way violates the therapist-client trust.
- does not encourage you to participate in your own healing.
- always portrays you as the victim of others, not as someone who also can harm others:
- doesn't regularly participate in on-going professional education for himself or herself.
- encourages the use of alcohol to deal with your problems.
- prescribes drugs without explaining fully the reason for their use, their side effects, and alternative options.
- sees only negatives in your family or spouse

Interview your therapist before hiring him or her to assist you and husband in solving your problems connected to Baby Mama Drama. When you find a therapist who is happy to answer all of your pre-session questions and meets your criteria then say a prayer and make an appointment. It just may bring you and your husband closer and could possibly save your marriage.

❖ENCOURAGE THROUGH LOVE AND REMAIN AS ONE

You and your husband must keep each other motivated to face all of life's challenges, not just the curveballs that BM throws at you. What about your dreams, your careers, your goals and wishes? You and your husband must nurture your spirits so that BM's drama becomes but a speck on your canvas.

Praise Hubby's Talents: Does your husband have talents that he could develop further? Encourage him to take a class or begin a new career. Purchase books for him that celebrate the things he likes to do, whether it be fishing, cooking, buying and selling real estate or learning new languages. Make your husband feel as if you think he can climb the highest mountain with his intelligence and diligence. You'll see how much your husband's energy level will flourish, which means good news for your family in so many ways.

Tell Him He's a Good Dad: Your husband might feel as if he is to blame for BM's presence in your life. It's true that if BM were a nicer person, things would be a lot easier when it came to your husband's co-parenting relationship with her and your relationship with the stepchildren. But it's BM's job to improve her life, as it is your job to improve yours. Tell your husband that you do not blame him for BM's behavior. Let him know that it isn't his fault if his children don't respect you the way you would like them to. Tell your husband what a loving, wise and caring father he is to those children—chances are no one else is telling him. Why not be the one person to uplift him? Show him that you respect and admire his parenting abilities.

Pray Together When You Can: Whatever spiritual path you follow with your husband should be a tool to bring you closer and through any adversity. Even if you only have time to say a few spiritual words or prayers upon wakening or at the dinner table it will benefit you to share this time and energy together. Ask your Creator to bless your family, your children and to give you the strength to face all trials, including BM's tirades and ill behavior. Make sure you thank your Creator for blessing you with all of the positive things you have, too. Give thanks for your home, your education, your babies, your car, your telephone service and whatever else you are thankful for. Life will be more colorful and abundant for you and your husband.

Spend Time Together, No Children Allowed: When was the last time you dressed up and looked fine for your husband? When was the last time you went and had a nice dinner by candlelight while listening to a live jazz band? Buy tickets to a rare Japanese dance performance or see a play at your city's grandest theater. You and your husband need a chance to experience the fruits of your labor and one of those is leisurely time together. Give yourselves a chance to look in each other's eyes without interruption. Join the rest of the world's lovers and celebrate the blessing of your bond.

Befriend Other Positive Couples: It will really help you and your husband to stay inspired by surrounding yourselves with other couples who highly value their relationships. There's a really infectious and good feeling you and your husband will receive from being in the presence of loving couples. This also gives you a chance to share your happiness with others who will be happy for you. Invite a positive couple over for dinner or a Saturday barbeque and have a good time over great laughs and stimulating conversation.

Be Gentle: A professor I know taught a class with her husband. I was amazed at how well they gelled and reflected each other's warm personas. Their connection was so natural that I assumed they must have known each other for years. During a bathroom break, and with a tinge of jealousy, I told her what a nice couple they made. I, too, hoped to evolve with my husband in a similar way. She told me that it was a second marriage for both of them and that their secret formula was treating their marriage "gently." I took her advice and became a better wife that day as a result. Treat your husband gently so that he will in turn treat you the same way. Apologize when you're wrong, let him know that you're open to discuss problems, smile at him for no reason and don't wait for him to request his favorite dinner. Cradle your marriage. It is your precious jewel and it is priceless.

As long as you and your husband remain considerate of one another and realistic about your situation you will be able to move forward together. No one else can force you to work as a team. Both of you are responsible for finding efficient and fresh ways to preserve and enjoy your marriage.

3

lady goldfinger: the money-hungry baby mama

❖CHILD SUPPORT: YOUR HUSBAND'S GOTTA PAY IT

Okay so BM can't really afford the shiny car that's she's driving. She still lives with her mama, or else refuses to move out of the roach-infested apartment in which your stepchildren live. BM gets her nails done yet spends no money on educational enrichment for your stepchildren. BM parties and leaves her children with anyone who will watch them or else leaves them by themselves if they're old enough to dial 911.

And even though BM may socially, educationally and emotionally neglect her children she *does* pride herself on being dedicated to dressing them in the latest Polo, Coogie, Gap, Timberland boots, DKNY sweaters and Reebok sneakers. BM takes no time to pursue activities of a more intellectual kind for her children. Do they know who Jacob Lawrence, Pablo Picasso or Vincent Van Gogh are? Of course not, using money to enroll her children in a weekend art class wouldn't cross BM's mind. Have they been registered for an S.A.T. prep course? Nah, BM has no desire to pay "all that money for some stupid class." For all I know your stepchildren may have no idea who Malcolm X is, but know how to do the Harlem shake until their shoulders get dislocated. I don't have anything against dancing or having fun, but shouldn't children be given a bit more for their minds to chew? Basically your husband's money is being used to fund a sad cycle that BM will never advance beyond. It's a shame isn't it?

Get over it now.

Any decent person would agree that child support should be used, stretched and manipulated in whatever way possible so that the children receiving it will be afforded a higher quality of life. Hopefully BM will use the child support not only to buy nutritious groceries, but also to save toward a bigger house or safer apartment. Maybe BM will use the money to help further her education so that she can make a lucrative career move that in the end will benefit her children. Yet many wives and their husbands are puzzled to see how BM overlooks her children for nonsensical and petty purchases.

Let me repeat myself. Please get over it now.

My husband gives his children money so that they will hopefully have a better life under the care of BM. This makes sense to me. Whatever BM decides to do with the money is none of my business unless it is causing illegal harm to my husband's children. It's great that my husband is willing to financially support the children he created, but many times we were flabbergasted with the standards under which his children were living: physically, socially, culturally and mentally. Once I realized that I had no control over BM's financial decisions or how much the courts said that my husband should pay, I let go of many of my judgments and thanked my Creator that my parents raised me with the right tools to be what I considered a good mother to any children that I would give birth to in the future.

Does that mean that as a wife you won't have an opinion about what BM does with your husband's money? Surely you still will have your ideals, but as long as child support is mandatory the custodial parent (in many cases a BM) will make the final spending choices for that allotted money. Stop obsessing and worrying about it. BM gets the money, BM spends it and the stepchildren get the quality of life they get.

In every state there are guidelines or an equation that a court follows to come up with the amount of money your husband must financially contribute toward his children from a previous relationship. You or your husband may think that this amount is too much or unfair. Well, you've both got two choices.

One: You can give up the next five years of your professional careers and lobby your state senate and assembly to make fairer financial adjustments and hold BMs accountable for spending child support in a decent manner. Or if you're really incensed to a maniacal level, you can resent the fact that the children were ever born and hope that something horrible happens to BM for taking the money that is "yours."

Two: You can accept what the child support mandate is and then continue focusing on being the successful and supportive couple that you both are. You can continue to excel in your career, spend *your* household's money the "right way" and hope that BM gives the children a good life with the money that your state awards them with each month.

I chose option two, but by all means if you and your husband have the energy to attempt getting your state's guidelines changed, write a book and I'll be the first to buy it! I'm not belittling those fathers and their wives or partners who do write state officials to make a difference, but in reality it is an uphill battle that will take a lot of time, dedication and hope.

What I am saying is that your life shouldn't be wrapped around trying to change what is inevitable. Child support is inevitable. The amount of money that is ordered is flexible depending on your husband's financial makeup, but you must both really evaluate if going back and forth to court over a few dollars will be worth it in the long run. Think about the costs of hiring a lawyer for an amount of money that may well exceed the money you will have shaved off of child support. Maybe you're willing to pay these extra legal fees because you firmly believe that BM shouldn't get a penny more than what is owed to the children. Or you may be on the other side of the fence and simply hope that the extra financial cushion you provide BM with will mean a better life for the children.

You must accept child support as you accepted your husband's children. Your stepchildren would not be getting the extra perks that they've received if your husband didn't help their mother keep the lights on or gas in her car. He's not doing it for BM, he's paying out of responsibility to his children. Be thankful that your hubby can claim this good deed.

BM may never, ever thank him for this. She may never appreciate how hard your husband works so that her children can receive nicer birthday presents, spending money on class trips or extra long johns during the winter. But child support payments only buy things like food, fun and life's necessities. It won't buy a miracle and turn BM into a grateful mom who splurges on educational toys instead of her ever-expanding bootleg movie collection.

Again, you do have two choices on how to handle the child support that your husband is bound by law to pay to his children. Don't obsess over it and drown in endless conversation over how much money BM is wasting. Just make sure that your house's financial setup is solid.

❖DON'T BE ROBBED!

Just because the state has guidelines for child support payments doesn't mean that you and your husband shouldn't become familiar with certain legal terms and laws that affect your bank account. Educate yourself because you are an investor in your family. In the end you should know into which channels the incoming salaries of your household flow. Your husband should especially be an expert in the area of child support because this is an important part of being a responsible husband to you.

We already know that some BMs are so miserable that they spend much of their time trying to avenge themselves by hurting your husband. If he is emotionally and financially stable then that makes him even more of a tempting target to a money-hungry BM. Some BMs will lie or provide false documents in family court to make it appear as her income is less than what it really is. The purpose of this is to make the courts place more of the financial burden on your husband. We as wives don't want to see anyone violate our husbands, emotionally or financially. That's why it is important for you as a wife to learn the guidelines of your state so that you can help support your husband if BM takes him to court.

You don't have to be your husband's lawyer, but you should encourage him to seek the advice of a lawyer, a financial planner and a certified professional accountant. If you have to help him pay for consultations or legal fees and it is not a burden on you, then you should help your husband attain these services. The information and guidance you'll get from these professionals will leave both of you more educated and confident about the decisions that are made when hubby's child support is determined.

If you notice that your husband is not diligent in seeking information to protect his financial assets then you need to understand why. Hubby may feel overwhelmed at having to become a scholar on child support terminology and custodial law, but he must understand that while it is his duty to financially support his children it is also his duty to financially support you and whatever lifestyle and dependents both of you share. Just as you are expected to be a stepmother, he should be expected to pursue the best financial standards that he can for the sake of the family that you have given him, whether it is just the two of you or whether you also have children together.

Sometimes the courts can make mistakes in assessing court support orders. If your husband suspects this he should make arrangements to have an audit done by the court that issued the order. Basically an audit will force the child support collection office to retrace the calculations of the child support order and make sure that your husband was not overcharged. Your husband will have to check with your area's family court to find out how to request an audit.

❖YOUR MONEY IS YOUR MONEY

It's true. Some BMs will have the audacity to try getting their hands on your money because they are angry or jealous of your relationship and standard of living with your husband. BM may believe that if you and your husband are going to be happy and in love—then she'll see to it that you're broke, too. BM can't and will never be able to control how financially well off you and your husband are and she's in for a big disappointment if she thinks she's entitled to your money.

Rarely is a wife's salary used to fund a child support order for her stepchildren. If you and your husband decide to have children of your own and your husband returns to court for a downward modification in child support, then your salary may be taken into consideration. In many U.S. states your husband will get a modest decrease in child support payments, but the judge may want to know how much you are making to support your child. In other words, if BM is expected to work to help support her biological children, then the same rules apply to you, the wife. That's why the court is interested in seeing how much money will be available to the children that you will have with your husband.

Note that not all states will ask for a wife's financial information if her husband seeks a downward modification due to the birth of a new child. Also, in some states there isn't even a downward modification given to husbands who have a new baby to support. You really must familiarize yourself with your state's child support guidelines and laws in order to make a solid financial plan for your family.

Just because BM works or does not work to support your stepchildren doesn't mean that you have to follow her footsteps. The court can't force you to put your baby in daycare and work a fulltime job. The court can't force you to become a stay-at-home mother, either. That choice is between you and your husband. Some wives decide that they can run a household and raise children off of their husband's salary while other wives choose to keep even more income rolling into the home by pursuing a career.

My husband and I decided that we could afford for me to be a stay-at-home mother to our daughter until I was ready to join the workforce again. But you may decide that you don't want to stay at home, you'd rather keep the flow of income at its optimum level. Only you can decide what choice makes the most sense for your family. Either way, you and your husband must decide how your family will stay financially afloat. You'd have to make these decisions whether there was a BM in your life or not.

Here is an abridged glossary of child support terms. You can find the full glossary in Appendix A.

Accrual

Sum of child support payments that are due or overdue.

Alleged Father

A person who has been named as the father of a child born out of wedlock, but who has not been legally determined to be the father; also referred to as putative father.

Arrearage

Past due, unpaid child support owed by the non-custodial parent. If the parent has arrearages, s/he is said to be "in arrears."

Case

A collection of people associated with a particular child support order, court hearing, and/or request for IV-D services. This typically includes a Custodial Party (CP), a dependent(s), and a Non-custodial Parent (NCP) and/or Putative Father (PF). Every child support case has a unique Case ID number and, in addition to names and identifying information about its members, includes information such as CP and NCP wage data, court order details, and NCP payment history.

Child Support

Financial support paid by a parent to help support a child or children of whom they do not have custody. Child support can be entered into voluntarily or ordered by a court or a properly empowered administrative agency, depending on each State's laws. Child support can involve cases where:

> IV-D cases, where the custodial party (CP) is receiving child support services offered by State and local agencies; (such services include locating a non-custodial parent (NCP) or putative father (PF); establishing paternity; establishing, modifying, and enforcing child support orders; collecting distributing, and disbursing child support payments).

> IV-A cases, where the CP is receiving public assistance benefits and the case is automatically referred to the State Child Support Enforcement CSE) Agency so the State can recoup the cost of the benefits from the non-custodial parent (NCP) or defray future costs.

> IV-E cases, where the child(ren) is being raised not by one of their own parents but in the foster care system by a person, family, or institution and the case is also automatically referred to the CSE to recoup or defray the costs of foster care.

Non IV-D orders, where the case or legal order is privately entered into and the CSE is not providing locate, enforcement, or collection services (called); often entered into during divorce proceedings.

The support can come in different forms, including:

> Medical support, where the child(ren) are provided with health coverage, through private insurance from the non-custodial parent (NCP) or public assistance that is reimbursed whole or in part by the NCP, or a combination thereof.

> Monetary payments, in the form of a one-time payment, installments, or regular automatic withholdings from the NCP's income, or the offset of State and/or Federal tax refunds and/or administrative payments made to the NCP, such as Federal retirement benefits.

Child Support Enforcement (CSE) Agency

Agency that exists in every State that locates non-custodial parents (NCPs) or putative fathers (PF), establishes, enforces, and modifies child support, and collects and distributes child support money. Operated by State or local government according to the Child Support Enforcement Program guidelines as set forth in Title IV-D of the Social Security Act. Also known as a "IV-D Agency".

Custodial Party (CP)

The person who has primary care, custody, and control of the child(ren).

Custody

Legal custody is a determination by a court which establishes with whom a child will live. Physical custody describes with whom the child is living regardless of the legal custody status. Joint custody occurs when two persons where legal and/or physical custody of the child(ren). Split custody occurs when 2 or more children from the same person are in the legal custody of different people.

Custody Order

Legally binding determination that establishes with whom a child shall live. The meaning of different types of custody terms (e.g., Joint Custody, Shared Custody, Split Custody) vary from State to State.

Non-custodial Parent (NCP)

The parent who does not have primary care, custody, or control of the child, and has an obligation to pay child support. Also referred to as the obligor.

Wage Withholding

A procedure by which scheduled deductions are automatically made from wages or income to pay a debt, such as child support. Wage withholding often is incorporated into the child support order and may be voluntary or involuntary. The provision dictates that an employer must withhold support from a non-custodial parent's wages and transfer that withholding to the appropriate agency (the Centralized Collection Unit or State Disbursement Unit). Also known as income withholding.

For more terms see the Child Support Glossary at the back of this book in Appendix A.

❖REACHING YOUR OPTIMUM FINANCIAL STATUS

It's true that if your husband didn't have to pay child support, you and he might be able to save more money, go on lengthier vacations or afford a fancier car. Many wives in your predicament fantasize endlessly about how the absence of BM would mean a more financially comfortable life. Wives would probably be more understanding if they didn't have to deal with the tricks and lies of spiteful money-hungry BMs, so you can't really blame them for dreaming.

But what happens when reality takes center stage? You and your husband are still scorned by BM and the child support MUST be paid. In the long run it is a waste of your energy to look upon child support as a dark cloud hanging over your head. It may be a burden inside your idealistic world, but it helps clothe, feed and shelter your husband's children. Even though they may not realize it or BM may trash your husband's name and his efforts to these children, your husband's money is one of the best provisions they could receive.

So why do you still believe that you and your husband are being shortchanged or robbed? Could it be that you and your husband are not living up to *your* financial abilities? Are you hesitant about starting your own business or changing to a more lucrative career? Is your husband reluctant to take on a second job temporarily in order to save more money? Are you living above your means and frivolously spending money that could be invested or saved?

There are a variety of sources that will help you and your husband plan a sound budget and savings plan for your household. You and your husband can enjoy vacations, a shinier car and a bigger house if you focus on your finances rather than on how BM spends child support.

Take some time out of your schedules and meet to discuss the monthly financial flow and decide what changes need to be made to improve your credit, spending habits, etc. Consider taking charge of debts and working out payment plans to eliminate them. A financial planner can help you take steps in the right direction.

If you focus on what you don't have because of child support, then you'll waste a lot of time that could be spent planning the solid financial future that you and your husband can have together. It's true that BM might think that the grass is greener on your husband's side of the fence, and maybe it is. It is up to her to improve her financial standing, as child support can only do so much. It is also up to you and your husband to take the bull by the horns and decide how you will attain the standard of life you desire.

You can do it, trust me, child support payments can't make you poor or rob you of a better life, only your negative thinking and victimized thinking can!

- Set up meetings with your husband so that you can both explore ways that you can improve your family's financial status.

- Don't be afraid to focus on a higher-paying career or an entire career change, the monetary incentive may be well worth it.

- Focus on how you and your husband can pay off debts and improve your credit.

- Be more disciplined with your spending habits. Live within your means so that one day you can attain better living standards.

- Don't focus on how much more BM has as a result of child support payments

- Focus on the higher incomes that you and your husband can bring in to your household.

- Utilize your talents, education and interests to reap a better life.

- Consider a financial planner to point you in the right direction for investing and saving.

❖PITY THE MONEY-HUNGRY BM

BM no longer has control in your husband's life. Your husband is not fooled by games she plays with their children. BM has shown her lack of integrity and sanity, which has only left her in a deeper funk, frustrated that she has no way of truly affecting your happiness.

If BM uses their children or state-mandated child support as a way to emotionally ruin your husband then it will probably be a long time until she feels victorious. There is no amount of money that can change a vicious or bitter person's thinking. If BM is constantly trying to act out her anger toward your husband by threatening to financially rape him, then the joke's on her. Clearly, she is not motivated to live up to her optimal financial status for the sake of her own dignity and her children. The only word to describe a life planned in this way is pathetic.

True BM may use your husband's hard-earned money to get a manicure or to take her new boyfriend on a vacation but you nor your husband can control this. BM draws up the blueprint for her life. Maybe she will actually save some of the child support and supply the children with a new, bigger home. If she does this to show your husband that she can make it without him then that is her issue. BM must do what she feels is fulfilling and if she thinks that making wise financial choices will enrage you and your husband then so be it.

Only BM can learn that child support payments are but a small factor in the whole scheme of life. Chances are by the time she realizes that her anger was never healed through endless court battles for money or misuse of child support—the children will be near emancipation age or child support payments will have ended.

BM can't punish you financially for falling in love with a man and marrying him. Your destiny, your marriage and your happiness are really none of this woman's business although she believes you have taken her potential for happiness away. She may, in her idiocy, believe that if a judge raises child support that somehow you and your husband will end up on the road to a homeless shelter. Yet the only thing she'll see is that you and your husband are constantly improving the quality of your life, your relationship and neither of you are hardly breaking a sweat over the mandated support payments she receives from your household.

Pity BM for her lack of motivation in all areas of life. Pity BM for the intense anger she has toward you and your husband. Pity BM for fighting a losing battle.

No child support check, only divine intervention, can help her heal and desist with planning your family's financial demise.

4

no home training:
tales of a rude ex

❖WHAT IS HER PROBLEM?

Your beauty, grace and intelligence don't sit well with BM. Why shouldn't she try to constantly offend you? BM must find some way to satiate her emptiness and you are the perfect target.

Why is BM relentlessly rude toward you? She wants to push your buttons so that you can either leave your husband and his Baby's Mama Drama behind *or* react to her in such a way that she is satisfied at the level of discomfort, intimidation or frustration she has attempted to fuse into your life. BM deliberately tries to upset you by pulling out a hat of the ugliest tricks complete with rolling eyes, obscenities and utter lack of self-respect. That's why you're going to learn how to ignore her, as she constantly proves to you that she is not worthy of being acknowledged.

I remember the first time I met BM. I knew my husband, whom I was dating at the time, had children and naturally a BM was connected to him. I had no problem reaching out in a confident manner and shaking BM's hand. To this day, I beam with delight when I recall how much of a lady I have always been throughout BM-related challenges, but it has been a Herculean task at times.

Have you tried starting off on the right foot but noticed that no matter how cordial, polite, patronizing and accommodating you were there was always the lingering scent of BM's funky attitude? In addition to holding yourself back from smacking BM whenever she spoke to your husband in a rude, outlandish tone, you also began to notice that BM took extra strides in directing nasty comments or behavior toward you.

You may have experienced some of these things:

- Unusually prolonged stares from BM when your husband drops off/picks up the visiting stepchildren.

- If you say hello to BM or try to make small talk her responses are harsh or non-existent.

- BM calls your home and refuses to politely ask to speak with your husband or her children if they are visiting.

- BM tells your in-laws horrible lies about you.

- BM tells your stepchildren that they don't have to listen to you or follow your household's rules.

You may be thinking *Why me? If BM has a problem, she needed to settle that score with my husband a long time ago, he's the one that's connected to her, not me!* This is a sound premise but if you're reading this book then you should know by now that BM is no pacifist philosopher intrigued with logic.

In BM's twisted mind, YOU are the outsider. YOU are the enemy. In fact, BM probably believes YOU put an ancient African spell on your husband so that he would marry you—because it is YOU who has stolen him from her and their children, right? BM believes that bearing your husband's children gives her the right to own their father and to own his future. Maybe in a fairytale but in real life, all men and women stand the chance of losing a partner for a myriad of reasons.

BM will do her best to isolate you from the stepchildren, from your husband and even the extended family. You may feel like a worker ant in your queendom instead of the queen, but don't let this fool make you take off your crown for a Battle Royale. Instead you must allow her to fumble mindlessly into the moat and drown in her own foolishness.

Rule Number One: BM has a right to be an (you can insert insult of your choice, mine follows) irrational, idiotic nuisance.

This is the one thing that many wives fail to remember about difficult BMs. These women had certain issues and deficiencies before we met them. They were rude, they were liars and they were inconsiderate. What makes you think that your presence mandates a change in BM? Accept that this is the kind of person she is. Let's look at a few ways we can begin to effectively ignore her with the following exercise. You can also enlarge a copy of the following worksheets and share it with a friend who's struggling with Baby Mama Drama, too.

Worksheet: BM has a Right to Be Herself

List five rude and disgusting traits you've noticed about BM:

1. _____
2. _____
3. _____
4. _____
5. _____

Now look over these behaviors and then answer these questions.

Did you have anything to do with raising this woman from childhood?

Do you think that you actually have the power to change her personality?

Do you have the time or desire in your days to schedule solutions on how teach an uncouth, grown woman how to behave in an acceptable manner?

You may laugh at these questions, but think about what I'm asking. If you have nothing to do with BM's lack of class, then why spend so much of your energy complaining or reacting to her foolishness? You must learn to focus on the things that truly matter in your life, and although BM has made a voodoo doll with your face on it there's no need for you to focus on her the way she has focused on you. Too many wives remain stuck and puzzled with BM's behavior. It's truly a waste of time.

List five positive things about your personality that make you proud of yourself:

1. _____
2. _____
3. _____
4. _____

5. _____

Remember these five traits. These are the weapons you will use when you encounter BM's annoying rudeness. Let's say you listed **intelligence** as one of your strong points. You obviously pride yourself on academic achievement. You will train yourself to use your **intelligence** as a way of not letting BM's nastiness permeate your life.

For example: BM rolls her eyes and sucks her teeth whenever she sees you. As an **intelligent** person, you are gifted with understanding beyond the average person, are you not? Your **intelligence** should lead you to know that reacting to BM's teeth-sucking would be an insult to the usage of your highly-toned brain cells. The day that BM can invent a mathematical equation proving that the laws of nature bind you to allotting her any significant attention is the day that you, an **intelligent** woman, might give her a second glance. And as always remember rule number one: BM has the right to be who she is.

Now list three things that BM has done that have offended you:

1. _____
2. _____
3. _____

Remember that just because BM reserves the right to be ignorant doesn't mean you must tolerate her nonsense. Your objective is to PRESERVE THE BEAUTY OF WHO YOU ARE. Your objective is NOT TO CHANGE BM. Think about how you reacted to BM's nasty behaviors listed above. Were you graceful? Were you intimidated? Were you piping mad? Did you give BM too much energy or did you leave her unsatisfied that you hardly gave her a second of your precious time?

Now fill in the following three statements. Use a separate piece of paper, or read them aloud to yourself. It will take some thinking, so don't rush.

> I am a woman who is *list one of your admirable traits.* When BM offended me by *fill in number 1 from the above list,* I *write down what your reaction was and how you handled the situation.*

Now use either one of these statements to complete the lesson.

a. As a *list one of your admirable traits* woman, I am proud of the way I reacted. I did not try to change her, but I did not give her anything she did not deserve. I preserved my *list one of your admirable traits,* not to prove anything to BM, but because naturally, I'm damned good, gifted and graceful in executing my *list one of your admirable traits.* I didn't like what BM did, but she has a right to be who she is as long as she doesn't invade my personal or social space. I didn't raise her, don't live with her and can't change her.

b. As a *list your admirable trait* woman, I am ashamed of the way I reacted. I concentrated too much on trying to change BM through my reaction. It did not work and as a *list your admirable trait* woman, I gave her too much of my energy. I must remember that my only priority is to preserve my *list your admirable trait,* not to prove anything to a grown woman who I didn't raise. I didn't like what BM did, but she has a right to be who she is as long as she doesn't invade my personal or social space. The next time BM *fill in number 1 from the above list,* I will use my *list your admirable trait* and *list a corresponding action that is better than what you initially did.* I didn't raise her, don't live with her and can't change her. Even though I could have acted differently, BM can not take away my *list your admirable trait.* I am entitled to make mistakes and learn from them.

You can write the statements in your journal and fill them in whenever BM tries to (or actually does) push your buttons. You will eventually learn to preserve your own positive traits rather than trying to change BM's behavior.

❖ LEARN TO RELAX WHEN CONFRONTED WITH BM'S RUDE BEHAVIOR

When confronted or otherwise tested by BM, you will either be with or without your husband. You may feel more protected if your husband is with you, especially if you bump into BM unexpectedly. Whether your husband is present or not, your ultimate goal is to avoid embarrassing yourself and your family.

We all know that rude comments or gestures can instigate a physical fight. Don't even think about fighting with BM. Although the idea may be slightly pleasurable, the reality of rolling on the floor, getting scratched and throwing punches won't make for pleasant memories or a sound reputation. You really don't want to be that physically close to BM, do you?

It is normal for you to show signs similar to an anxiety attack if you know that BM will be in the same place as you. Here are some signs of discomfort that you may exhibit whenever BM is near you and your family:

• Quick and shallow breathing

• Clammy hands

• Increased heart rate

• Restlessness

• The feeling that you are trapped and want to escape or run away

• The feeling that you want to attack BM, almost in an animal-like fashion

• Your face may feel flushed, as if all the blood has rushed to your neck and head

It isn't fair that BM's behavior should have such a psychosomatic effect on you. Before you can even comprehend how to deal with BM's rudeness you must recognize how you usually react to her. Your presence may also have the same effect on BM, and she may not know how to control herself, thus her constantly sour disposition. You on the other hand, will learn how to control these reactions. Soon you'll notice a decrease in your discomfort whenever BM and you must share the same space.

BM has the right to be whoever and whatever she is, remember? This philosophy will help you to lower your expectations of BM in any situation. For instance, if you and your husband attend a school play that your stepdaughter is starring in, then don't expect BM to save you a seat or smile at you upon noticing your arrival. Expect to have an enjoyable time with your husband. Also expect to possibly encounter a less than mannerly BM, but do not make this anticipation the highlight of your evening.

If you and your husband attempt to give your stepdaughter flowers after the play, and as you walk up to the child BM is staring at you rudely, don't be so appalled. It is her nature, and you have your nature as well. Let her stare, and then either flash her your toothiest smile or don't acknowledge her at all. Let your husband give his words of praise to his daughter and carry on with the rest of your night as you leave BM standing there, possibly still with a snarl on her face.

We will also look at how to react if BM goes beyond dirty looks and says something rude to you. But the reason for this example was to show you just how easily you can bypass BM. I didn't say you could change her. Remember, it's about preserving your couth. **BM will always reserve the right to be who she is**.

Relaxation techniques and realistic thinking are great ways to move beyond BM's rudeness. Here are some great ways to calm yourself when you end up face-to-face with an incorrigible BM:

Quiet Your Mind

Sometimes the negative self-talk we feed ourselves can drown out any possibilities of remaining relaxed in a stressful situation. Wives set themselves up for a showdown with BM before even seeing her. Be realistic but don't barrage your mind with visions of being attacked by a vicious pit bull with a foul mouth and BM's face.

Focus On Breathing

Concentrate on how much you love yourself and empower your lungs to BREATHE! The moment you start feeling as if you are about to suffocate remember that you have just as much right to the earth's supply of oxygen as anyone else, including BM! Breathe in through your nose deeply, let the air caress your throat for a second and blow coolly out of your mouth. Do this in small sets of three or five.

Your Golden Anchor

Envision yourself as a powerful ship. You are anchored into the middle of the Atlantic Ocean on a calm day when all of a sudden an intense thunderstorm approaches. Visualize a solid gold anchor holding your ship steady throughout the lightening and the thunder. You want your ship to stay afloat. Your wonderful traits are your "golden anchor" and although the storm tries to sink and batter what is on the surface—the unseen core of your being is something so strong and determined that a master body builder couldn't bend or break it. You are untouchable and unsinkable. Let your anchor work for you.

Take A Bathroom Break

Take a quick trip to the ladies room. Excuse yourself and walk in your proudest stride toward the bathroom. Once you get in there take a good look in the mirror. You're beautiful, you have manners, you're attractive and YOU are not the rude beast on the prowl for a fight! Now that you know you're too exquisite to be holed up in the bathroom, step right back out there and shine your light on anyone in your path.

Say A Special Prayer

Is there a special prayer that you use whenever faced with a challenge? Whisper it to yourself or say it silently in your mind. Ask your Higher Power to be by your side as you are met with the challenge of possibly being offended by BM. Ask your Higher Power to protect and bless your beautiful traits, your nervous system and your body.

❖AT SOCIAL EVENTS, BE COOL

What better way to challenge an opponent than in front of an audience? Many wives and their husbands are reluctant to attend the same social function as BM for fear she will embarrass them or just ruin the whole experience. As a result family functions, holiday outings, trips to a store in BM's neighborhood or events that center on your stepchildren may be avoided because you'd rather stifle yourself than have a run-in with BM.

This kind of anxiety is understandable, but erasing yourself is not. First accept that BM's unpredictable, rude behavior would make many people uncomfortable. You are not weak or a coward because you wish to avoid an unpleasant scenario in public. Your lack of tolerance for BM's nasty behavior is low, as it should be.

Unless you are attending an event that BM is hosting you are NOT obligated to say one word to her. That's right. Not even a simple "hello." I can't tell you if the BM in your life is worthy of your "hello" because a rude BM will not know how to even appreciate something as simple as a traditional salutation. If your husband thinks it best not to have any verbal contact with BM, then it's best to forget about saying "Hello," "How are you?" and yes, even the "Good-bye."

If you're reading this chapter because the BM in your life is so belligerent that you want to avoid verbal linkage with her in all ways then it's best you not speak, in fact, pretend she didn't even make it to the affair or venue. If on the other hand BM is sane enough to not misinterpret the word "hello," then be cordial and extend the same greeting you'd give to the local butcher or supermarket cashier.

I've offered some general tips on how to handle the social pressures of ignoring BM, while trying to make the best of the event. I am offering advice based on a worst-case scenario where BM has established herself as totally disrespectful toward you and your husband. She should not have the privilege of pushing your buttons or engaging you in a public and embarrassing verbal exchange. Here are the most common venues at which you may bump into your rude BM.

School Events (PTA night, seasonal plays, graduations)

This is an unfortunate situation where it would obviously benefit your stepchild to see all of the concerned adults in her life unite for the sake of encouraging and supporting her. With a rude BM, however, there are liabilities. You and your husband don't want to be embarrassed in front of your stepchild's principal, teachers or peers. BM doesn't care about embarrassing herself so why take any chances?

At school plays and graduations arrive early enough to find comfortable seats. Ideally you should put some distance between your seats and BM's. It's an event that you and your husband should enjoy, not endure. Don't put yourself in a position to fend off BM's dirty looks or snide comments, especially if you'd be tempted to react.

Make sure that you find out in advance where you and your husband can congratulate or mingle with your stepchild after the event. If there is a post-performance or family meeting area, go and wait for your husband's child with him. If BM is adamant about not welcoming you it doesn't matter because she isn't hosting the event.

At an appropriate time your husband should approach your stepchild and you should follow his lead. Don't stand off in a corner like some outcast. Both of you should then congratulate your stepchild, offer your presents, hugs, kisses, jokes, etc.

If possible, beforehand, your husband should make arrangements to take the child to dinner or lunch at a time that doesn't interfere with BM's plans. Obviously your husband will have to find out from BM or a reliable source if there are any such plans.

Don't linger too long, as you may notice your stepchild becoming uncomfortable under the pressure of being surrounded by adults she probably knows are at odds. If there are no important announcements or highlights following the event, you and your husband should prepare to leave the venue. Your objective was to show support and encouragement for the stepchild, and not to waste time tiptoeing around a BM who is a social time bomb.

If you are attending a parent-teacher conference with or without your husband, your objective is to speak with the teacher, any other school staff that you deem important and to get pertinent information regarding the stepchild's progress. If you like, ask about school notices, lunch menus or upcoming field trips or contests. These are you and your husband's only goals. If BM attends the school conference, this should not interfere with your ability to take care of business.

If your husband can't even take a chance on talking to his child's teacher with BM, then don't approach the teacher if BM engages him or her before you and your husband have your chance. Take a look around your stepchild's classroom. Take note of the textbooks, displayed schoolwork and art. You and your husband can even leave the classroom and lounge in the refreshment area or seek out other important school staff with whom you'd like to speak. It is a nuisance that the teacher will have to repeat herself about the progress of one child, but chances are the teacher would prefer repetition versus a nasty verbal exchange between BM, you and your husband.

If BM decides to aggressively approach you and your husband for whatever reason, be prepared to allow your husband to reply to any questions and comments she may have. Chances are he will keep his answers terse, as he knows that BM is likely to disrespect him or you at any moment.

Should BM try to provoke you with a rude question or comment at any school event, you can either use a combination of wit and grace to supply her with a quotable answer OR you can tell her simply that you refuse to engage in such nonsensical banter. It should go without saying that you and your husband should promptly excuse yourselves from BM's presence if she verbally attacks either one of you.

At the end of the parent-teacher conference you and your husband should leave with what you came for: information pertaining to your stepchild's education. Let BM leave with whatever nastiness she was unsuccessfully able to share with your family.

Extended family functions (family reunions, funerals)

Extended family functions may seem a bit intimidating, especially if many of your in-laws are friendly with BM. Don't let BM's relationship with your mother or father-in-law or your husband's other family members fool you into taking her abuse or second-guessing your right to be treated with respect. She may be polite with the rest of the family, but if you and your husband have witnessed an ugly side of BM, then that's your reality and you have to protect your space and peace.

If there's no chance that BM and you can exchange a civil greeting, then by all means simply pretend she isn't there. Don't try to provoke her by interrupting her conversations with your husband's aunt or purposely bumping into her on your way to the coat closet. BM has a right to attend these family functions, the primary reason being that your husband's children have a right to enjoy and be around their relatives. Even if BM appears to "hang around" your husband's family, you nor your husband can take this choice away from her, no more than she can destroy your choice to ignore her at these functions.

No one wants to attend family events constantly looking over their shoulder or anticipating an unpleasant experience. You and your husband should attend his family events with the intent of having a grand ole' time! Do not focus on BM's presence the whole time you're there. You and hubby should take time to catch up with family members, little nieces and nephews who are growing up and getting taller or the elders who always have a great story to tell. Enjoying yourselves is your priority. Whatever BM's intentions are for attending the affair should not overshadow your experience.

Do you feel as if BM is competing with you for family affections? Maybe she is. But the one mistake you should not make is to enter this petty competition with BM. The only person you need to worry about impressing is your husband and the children you have together. Everyone else, including your stepchildren and your husband's extended family will most definitely have their opinions. Your energy is best reserved for being yourself and bonding with your husband's family. Dress the way you want to, cook and bring an unusual dish if you think your husband's family may enjoy it. Wear your hair the way you like it and leave the competitions to Miss America contestants.

Formal Events (city council meeting, family court)

This is one of the easier social situations for dealing with BM because there are actually vices to keep social order. BM is less likely to have an embarrassing outburst, make violent threats or attempt to go one on one with you in these arenas. This does not mean that BM will undoubtedly BEHAVE, it just improves the likelihood that she will.

If BM says anything directly to you in a family courtroom, for instance, the judge will probably direct her attention back to His Honor or the bailiff will take over. At a city council meeting or a local organization event, you would simply attend to your business and give BM little or no attention. Should she approach you in a less than desirable manner that makes you extremely uncomfortable then you should find a person at the event who is in charge of maintaining order. Ask this person to explain the rules of conduct for the event to BM. You nor your husband is a security guard or a police officer (and if you are, unless you're on duty, it isn't your job to teach a rude BM good behavior) but don't hesitate to ask one to put BM in check so that you can tend to your affairs.

In a nutshell, you really shouldn't have a problem with a rude BM at formal, non-family centered events because there is no social pressure for you to even acknowledge her. Just refrain from returning dirty looks if she throws them your way.

General Public Places (the supermarket, shopping mall, post office)

Here's where things can get a bit shaky if your BM is truly out to make an idiot of herself. Some wives actually live in the same neighborhood with a dreaded BM. This could be for a variety of reasons. Maybe the wife and husband are in the process of trying to move to another town or state, or maybe the husband wants to remain near his children for easier visitation. Either way, bumping into BM at the supermarket, mall or gas station doesn't have to turn into every wife's nightmare.

Here's a hypothetical situation. You're at the neighborhood dollar store and as you walk into the aisle for the paper plates and cups, you see BM at the other end. What should you do? Should you quietly and quickly turn around and make a beeline to the cash register to avoid BM seeing you? Maybe you should walk fiercely through the aisle and purposely let your basket knock her in the elbow and then dare her to say anything.

Well, you don't want to put off important errands *or* make yourself into a dollar store gangster on behalf of BM. What you want to do is continue down the aisle and select any items you are there to purchase. Yes, your heart may be beating a mile-a-minute and you may be praying to God that BM doesn't try to verbally assault you or ruin your day, but you have just as much right as she does to be in that aisle. So take your basket and walk that runway of disposable plates, cups and napkins as if you were the spokesperson for dollar stores across America.

If BM says something slick to you can either ignore her or respond with a slicker comeback of your own. THIS IS A TOUGH CHOICE TO MAKE. Before you decide to respond to BM, try to understand why you will do so. Is it to prove to BM that you aren't a pushover? Is it to put BM in her place once and for all? Here's some insight. There is a chance that accepting an invitation to BM's confrontational circus will let her know that you are no sappy, prim and proper pushover. There is a chance that standing up for yourself and using a few choice words will make BM back down. There is also the chance that your response will only add fuel to the fire.

If you have had all that you can take and absolutely feel that you must respond to a silly comment made by BM, it's quite understandable. Trust me, sometimes the Mask of Polite and Properly must come off, and I have taken it off when warranted. Did it change much about the BM in my life? Not really. Some BMs actually derive a masochistic pleasure from arguing with either the wife or the wife's husband. It's a call that only you can make.

Let's say that you decide to ignore her. It doesn't mean that you're a wimp. This route can convey a strong a message to BM. Basically you're saying, "I absolutely refuse to waste my verbal, analytical or cognitive skill on responding to your dumb ass." And the best thing is that you won't even have to say a word to get this message across, your indifference and silence speaks volumes.

❖KEEPING HER MADNESS OUT OF YOUR HOME

On the Phone: Maybe you and your husband have allowed BM to call your home for various reasons. However, you notice that she has absolutely no phone etiquette and doesn't understand that there is a proper way to conduct telephone conversation. In fact, she deliberately seems to use her worst social skills on the phone, especially when you answer.

First you and your husband have to decide whether or not BM's phone behavior is foul enough that you'd like to eliminate it from your lives. Then your husband should speak with BM and explain what is expected of her if she desires to have the privilege of calling your home. For example, your husband might tell BM that she is not to take up any issues regarding the children with you via telephone, and that she is to leave a message for him. Give BM a chance to show that she can follow you and your husband's rules. If her behavior improves, that's miraculous, so count your blessings. If her behavior stays the same or becomes even worse, then it's simple. Cut off her phone privileges.

You'll notice that there isn't a long section on this phone business. It simply isn't something you or your husband should put up with. After BM shows that she isn't capable of using a phone properly:

- Your husband or you at this point can tell her that she is not to call your home until you both give her written permission.

- You and your husband may send a written request to BM's home asking her not to call your home due to continual harassment/verbal abuse. For an extra kick you can get the letter notarized or have your lawyer send a letter.

- Arrange a voicemail box for BM to call and leave messages, your husband can then check the voicemail and return BM's calls. It's also handy because your husband can save/record any inappropriate messages that BM leaves for legal purposes.

- Your husband can request that BM only correspond with him via certified mail or email.

It's no mysterious puzzle. If BM is interrupting your days and nights with her ranting, raving and rude behavior then you don't have to tolerate it.

Unannounced Visits: My philosophy is that your home is the one place on this planet that you have the absolute right to peace of mind and safety. Although we all want to create some type of personalized nirvana behind the doors of our residences, there will be challenges that will infringe upon your desire to maintain this peace. Every now and then some deranged BM believes that she can get away with coming to your home, unannounced and with a bag of drama.

You'll notice that this section won't be lengthy either because tolerating a crazy trespasser holds no justification in my book. It doesn't matter what BM's reason is for coming across town or across state lines to your doorstep. If you nor your husband wants her arriving at your home unannounced (or at all) you need to tell her.

Your husband should be the person to explain this thoroughly to BM if possible. If your husband is unavailable to express this, then by all means, it is your home and you have every right to tell BM that she needs to receive written or verbal permission from either you or your husband before she comes nonchalantly knocking at your door.

Why do some BMs bring their wretched behinds to otherwise happy homes of married couples? The reasons BM would give are probably flimsy and illogical. The truth is that most times, BM wants an opportunity for conflict with either you or your husband. Some BMs are so driven to draw blood that they could care less if their own children witnessed them in a nasty verbal or physical altercation with you. Yes you…

Maybe BM wants to see what a great interior decorator you are. It could be that BM wants to intimidate you by trespassing, hoping that you'll be traumatized knowing she may come knocking at your door at anytime. BM may want to stir up trouble between you and your husband. The possibilities are endless but the bottom line is that you should not tolerate this kind of disrespect. Here are your options:

- Your husband must tell BM that she is not welcome to arrive unannounced at your home.

- If your husband is unavailable, you can feel free to tell BM yourself. Stay calm and business like, and don't indulge BM in any further conversation. She may be eager to pick a fight.

- After you and your husband have verbally requested that BM not come to your home, it would be wise to send her a written letter stating the same. For more clarity you can even attach copies of your town's ordinances that apply to trespassing. Check with your local police department and city/town hall clerk to get more information.

- Keep written records of each time BM has trespassed on your property and of each time you have requested that she cease. If you must later involve the courts or law enforcement agencies, bring these records to prove that BM was purposely harassing you and your husband.

- Your husband can attempt to get a restraining order, or if possible, you may be able to get an anti-harassment order.

- As much as you may want to, do not physically attack or harm BM for coming on your property, and only use physical force upon her as a method of self-defense.

- Call the police immediately if BM refuses to leave. It wouldn't hurt to call the police as soon as BM arrives; you'll probably want to make out a police report for your records anyway.

Yes, you must do a bit of record keeping and research so that the law will be on your side. It's your home and if you really don't want to see BM sniffing around on your front porch then you and your husband must show her that you mean business.

Time for a quiz! Now you know how to handle bumping into BM just about anywhere. Now take this quiz to see if you can apply your new-found knowledge.

1. BM will be at your mother-in-law's birthday party. You

    a. race frantically to the gym hoping to lose 15 pounds so that you can fit into a racy black mini. You'll be damned if BM steals the show from you.

    b. sigh and remind yourself that it'll be a challenge to attend, but since you've been focusing on limiting the amount of energy you give to BM, you don't sweat it.

    c. refuse to be in the same room as that trifling nutcase.

2. You and your husband are attending a city council meeting. BM happens to be there, too. As BM walks past you she shoots you a dirty look and then winks at your husband. You

    a. use this as the perfect opportunity to slip outside and slash BM's tires.

    b. loudly yell, "Who the hell are you winking at, you lowdown skeezer?"

    c. chuckle quietly to yourself and shake your head. You hope that one day her church sponsors her an exorcism, as she is obviously dealing with some demons.

3. Your husband's daughter is getting married. You are invited to the wedding, but the problem is that your husband's daughter wants him and BM to walk her down the aisle. You

    a. feel that your husband's daughter has every right to have her parents be there for her on her special day. You really are comfortable with her wishes.

    b. get into a nasty argument with your husband and threaten to divorce him if he walks down any aisle, at anytime, anyplace ever with BM.

    c.   fantasize about paying a street thug to break BM's legs, so that she'll look ridiculous hobbling down the aisle while you take numerous photos.

4.   After your stepson's piano recital, your husband wants to thank the piano instructor. BM is presently talking to the instructor. You

    a.   tell your husband that you're tired and don't feel like waiting.

    b.   insist that you and your husband interrupt BM, because she'll probably try to talk to the instructor all night. She's so inconsiderate.

    c.   sit with your husband and discuss the music program, you don't mind waiting patiently so that your husband can speak to the instructor. Fifteen minutes, however, is as long as you'll wait.

5.   You're at the local bank when BM walks in with your husband's 10-year-old daughter. You get along with your stepdaughter, but the last time BM called your home you got into an argument and nothing was resolved. You

    a.   make sure that before you leave you break your neck to say goodbye to your stepdaughter, BM's the one you can't stand.

    b.   discreetly wave to your stepdaughter and leave the bank after you see the teller.

    c.   break out into a sweat and immediately leave the bank, fearing that BM will try to intimidate or provoke you.

6.   Your three friends join you for dinner at a city restaurant. BM walks in with her latest boyfriend. You

    a.   realize that it's a free world and couldn't care less that BM is in the restaurant. As long as the hostess doesn't place her to sit near your table…

    b.   bribe one of the waiters to "accidentally" drop a plate of spaghetti on BM.

    c.   start ranting and raving to your friends about BM and her mission to make your life a living hell.

7. BM shows up unexpectedly at your home while your husband has visitation with their 12-year-old son. BM says that she needs to see her son immediately, and doesn't ask politely either. You

    a. look at her as if she's out of her mind before you proceed to slam the door in her face.

    b. tell her to wait outside, while you go and get your husband who is more than willing to explain clearly that BM is not to repeat this mistake again.

    c. go and get her son because you're so shocked you don't know what else to do.

8. Every time BM calls your home to speak with your husband she seems to lose all home training. No proper introduction, no greeting, just pure attitude and you've had enough. You

    a. burst into tears every time BM calls because you still don't understand why she is so unpleasant toward you.

    b. hang up on her every time.

    c. give your husband the phone, after you tell BM that in order to continue calling she'll have to adjust her tone.

9. Whenever your stepchildren call from BM's home, you can hear BM in the background. Usually she is saying a slew of offensive things about you or your husband. You

    a. tell your stepchildren to call back after their mother shuts up.

    b. ignore BM, but you do feel sorry that the stepchildren must live with such a person.

    c. ask your husband to confront BM about all of the horrible things she says about the both of you, even if she says them in her own house.

10. At a family barbeque that BM is attending also, your husband's nosy cousin points out to you that BM is telling everyone that your husband still thinks she has it going on. You see BM across the room schmoozing with your in-laws. You

    a. tell your cousin-in-law that you're enjoying the party, and that you'd rather taste test the potato salad instead of discussing BM.

b. realize that this is the perfect opportunity to beat up BM in front of your husband's family. When the old school classic "Set It Off" comes on, you set it off alright—with a left hook to BM's jaw.

c. ask with a quivering voice, "What else does that stupid liar say about my husband? Does she talk about me, too?"

Tally your score:
1) a-3, b-2, c-1; 2) a-1, b-3, c-2; 3) a-2, b-3, c-1; 4) a-1, b-3, c-2; 5) a-3, b-2, c-1; 6) a-2, b-3, c-1; 7) a-3, b-2, c-1; 8) a-1, b-3, c-2; 9) a-3, b-2, c-1; 10) a-2, b-3, c-1

Stop playing the victim (10–17)
Whenever BM walks into the room or calls your home, you freeze up or want to run away. Why? Do you think that she has more of a right to be on this planet than you do? You get offended easily by her nasty behavior and you let it cloud your self-esteem and your relationship with your husband. BM is the one with the problem, so why are you allowing her negativity to diminish you? The reason BM is so nasty toward you is that she can't stand the potentially powerful woman you truly are! Instead of shrinking every time BM invites you to a challenge, learn to stand tall and be an example of what a real woman should be. BM may not learn anything from your strengths, but at least you will be honoring yourself by walking tall and proud. You owe it to yourself to create a peaceful and satisfying life, so don't let BM fool you into living a life of chaos.

Why you always win (18–24)
Congratulations, it probably took some practice but you've mastered overcoming BM's constant rudeness. It hasn't been easy to stay poised, but the rewards are worth the effort. There have been a few times when you've had to shut BM down when she's attempted to go too far, but according to your discretion it was necessary. Most other times you couldn't care less if BM rolled her eyes to the back of her neck. You have more important things to concentrate on, and BM hates it that you don't shower her with your attention. You probably have a great spiritual foundation and an active lifestyle, which leaves more room to focus on things that really matter. Simply put, you're not her mama. Someone else will have to teach BM's about tact, manners and civility.

You're exhausting yourself (25–30)

First, take off the boxing gloves. Any little thing that BM does seems to make you extremely angry and annoyed, and you and your husband are no better off as a result. You must learn to accept that BM will continue being an embarrassment to herself. Don't fall into that same category by becoming a rabid, barbarian at her expense. There are so many other things that you could put your energy into, things that have probably suffered as a result of your misdirected focus on BM. Have you been to the gym lately? How about an African women's literature class at your local university? Have you done anything good for yourself or for your husband just because life is beautiful? You've wasted enough time on BM, it's time to get back to focusing on you.

Continue to reassess yourself by taking this quiz. When your score is between 18 and 24 you're moving in the right direction.

Remember it isn't your job to fix BM and turn her into a tolerable person. Don't accept blatant disrespect, but don't make it your mission to prove a point to BM by constantly reacting to her efforts. There's nothing a rude BM would like more than to know she got under the skin of a sharp woman like you.

It takes time to learn how to deal with BM's nasty looks, lies and off-the-wall comments. One moment you'll want to go buck wild on her and on other days you'll feel like running a thousand miles in the other direction. Sometimes the things BM will say are so unbelievably stupid you won't be able to do anything but laugh. You owe it to yourself to find a balance where you are brave enough to put BM in her place when the situation truly calls for it. But there will also be many times that BM deserves not an ounce of your attention. You will ease into the right gear, just give yourself a chance.

5

her middle name should have been psycho

❖YOU CAN CALL HER CRAZY

Okay so you're no shrink, but you know there's a difference between an unpleasant person and a derelict. You know there's a difference between, as James Brown put it, karate and crazy. It is certainly possible that the BM you are dealing with has a mental disorder and this puts you in a different ball game.

BM may have mental disorders that were shaped or in existence from her childhood. If she has never gotten professional help then I'm sure you and your husband are feeling the effects of her self-negligence. Many times wives repeatedly try to figure out the quirky behaviors, the mood swings and the erratic behaviors that some BMs display. These wives end up emotionally and mentally exhausted because they are searching for a rational explanation behind BM's behavior, when in fact, the only person who can offer a rational explanation is a psychologist or some other mental health expert.

Maybe BM appears to be unnaturally extroverted one minute and then paranoid the next. Maybe BM has extremely strange and bizarre ways of disciplining your stepchildren. BM may even have issues that result in her entertaining abusive boyfriends, which in the end will have an effect on your stepchildren, too. It could be that BM is the most shameless liar you've ever met. Does BM appear to be depressed all the time? Does she search for ridiculous ways to get attention? Is BM too attached to her children? Think of the things your BM has done that have left you baffled. There is simply no sane conclusion no matter how intelligent you think you are.

There are many things that may puzzle you and your husband, but you must take into consideration that BM may have some mental and emotional deficiencies that will never be healed without professional help. In other words, you really can't help or change BM, you can only live life with the knowledge that BM DOES need help—and it IS NOT your job to help her find it. That's a journey she will have to be brave enough to endure on her own.

❖Forms of Mental Disorders

These descriptions of mental illness symptoms are not an alternative to diagnosing BM, yourself or anyone else. For the fairest assessment of any individual a mental health professional should be consulted. I have, however, complied a list of common mental illnesses and their symptoms to give you an idea of the issues that BM *might* be afflicted with. These descriptions were compiled using the American Psychiatric Association's *Diagnostic and Statistical Manual of Mental Disorders*, the National Alliance for the Mentally Ill and other resources that you will find in the bibliography.

Bipolar Disorder

Also known as manic depression, bipolar disorder is a disorder that results in extreme mood shifts. It can last days or months.

Symptoms: When BM is on the high end of the bipolar disorder spectrum you may notice that she is in an extremely happy, elated mood sometimes, and then at other times she is highly irritable, angry and unpleasant. BM may talk faster than normal or show an abnormal increase in energy. BM may talk about making far-fetched, grand plans.

When BM goes to the low end of the spectrum she will appear depressed and indifferent to a variety of issues. BM will be inactive and irritable and prone to inverted, non-communicative behavior. She may even threaten suicide. Pessimism, feelings of worthlessness and living a very inactive life are also symptoms of the manic depression that accompanies bipolar disorder.

Major Depression

Women are twice as likely to be affected by depression. Appetite, sleep, mood and social behavior are all areas affected by major depression and one out of seven women will suffer this disorder at least once in her lifetime. BM's depression may also be seasonal, meaning that during a certain season, like winter, BM becomes very depressed.

Symptoms: BM may be constantly sad or anxious and unmotivated. She may constantly throw her failures in your husband's or your face or she may completely withdraw from both of you. BM will be irritable and will experience feelings of hopelessness and indecisiveness. You may notice that BM has either lost or gained a great amount of weight. She may threaten or hint at suicide

Anxiety Disorder

Anxiety disorders come in other forms known as panic disorder, post-traumatic stress disorder, phobias and generalized anxiety disorder. Many people suffer from a combination of anxiety disorders and it appears to run in families.

Symptoms of panic disorders: BM may have at least four or more panic attacks weekly. Sometimes panic attacks can be mistaken for heart attacks, heart disease or respiratory problems. These attacks are triggered by stress, hormonal imbalances or the use of drugs and alcohol.

Symptoms of phobias: BM has very strange fears of ordinary things and situations. With social phobia, BM is very afraid of looking silly or foolish in public, so she tends to alienate herself. With agoraphobia BM is afraid of being trapped in a situation, mainly a public place. And if BM falls in to the category of having specific phobia, she may fear anything from elevators to clowns. Phobias can also lead to depression.

Attention Deficit Disorder

If you notice that BM has a hard time paying attention, is hyper or impulsive then she may have attention-deficit/hyperactivity disorder (ADHD). Although this is a disorder associated with children, it is not limited to children and can remain with a person into adulthood.

Symptoms: BM may not be able to pay close attention to detail and often makes careless mistakes in all areas of her life. She may appear not to be listening when you or your husband try to speak to her. Following directions, organization and finishing projects are a challenge for BM. If there is a project that requires concentrated mental effort, BM will try to avoid engaging in it. She is forgetful and very careless.

You may also notice that BM has a habit of fidgeting with her hands, feet or squirms about when seated. BM probably is an excessive talker, who blurts outs answers before a question is even completed. Intruding and interruption are her forte, and she doesn't know how to wait her turn. When she engages in regular or leisure activities, she can't remain quiet or calm.

Borderline Personality Disorder

More women are diagnosed with this depressive disorder than men. BPD, said to border on schizophrenia, involves an unhealthy impulsive character and unstable mood. BM's self-image and personal relationships usually suffer as a result. BM's wacky moods and impulsive nature has probably left her at odds with many people, including family members. If BM has BPD, it could be traced back to her psychological development during childhood, or she may have been neglected or abuse during that time.

Symptoms: BM has inappropriate, intense and uncontrollable fits of anger. She spends money impulsively. BM may even use drugs, be promiscuous, drive recklessly, steal or overeat. BM is unsophisticated at analyzing her experiences with people and life; everything is either "good" or "bad." BM will try very hard to avoid abandonment, even if she is not in danger of being abandon by anyone. She is very insecure about her self-image, her long-term goals are unclear and her friendships are unstable.

Conduct Disorder/Adult Anti Social Personality Disorder

Conduct disorder means that the person affected does not know how to respect the rights of others and violates society's norms. As children, males are usually affected, with females being in the minority. A person with conduct disorder is always in trouble with authority figures, family members or peers and is prone to developing Adult Anti Social Personality Disorder. Although a tough image is represented the individual usually has very low self-esteem.

Symptoms: If BM is affected by either disorder you and your husband will observe that she often initiates physical fights and tries to bully, threaten or intimidate others. BM threatens to destroy or steal property. She may have even been found guilty of shoplifting, extortion or forgery. In other words, BM pretty much operates as a lying, violent criminal. BM believes she doesn't have to follow any rules, has no regard for authority and at the height of anger will resort to violent threats and animalistic behavior.

BM may stay out late at night, without regard to her children and their welfare. The abuse of alcohol or drugs may be present in BM's daily life. In many cases, the traits of BM's conduct disorder can be seen developing in her children. The disorder is exacerbated or initially encouraged by sexual, physical or emotional abuse, a learning disorder or a chaotic environment.

Dependent Personality Disorder

People with this disorder have an excessive need to be taken care of by others. They exert submissive, clingy behavior and have an intense fear of separation.

Symptoms: BM may have difficulty making everyday decisions without an excessive amount of advice and reassurance from other people. She may also seek out a romantic relationship as a source of care and support when any other kind of close relationship ends. She needs others to assume responsibility for most of the major areas in her life.

Narcissistic Personality Disorder

This disorder involves individuals who have a lack of empathy for others and a need for constant admiration.

Symptoms: BM may exaggerate her achievements and talents when speaking to others. She believes that she should be shown especially favorable treatment and that everyone should abide by her wishes. She fantasizes about unlimited power, beauty and success. BM is also envious of others or believes that everyone is envious of her. She doesn't know how to consider the feelings and needs of others if it conflicts with her arrogant philosophies.

Pathological Lying

If you find that BM effortlessly tells the most audacious, vicious or even unnecessary lies, then she may be a pathological liar. This is a personality and social disorder. BM may tell so many lies that you and your husband have given up on believing anything that she says. She may lie to get what she fervently believes she deserves, and will insist that her lie is truth even when confronted with reality. BM could be in fear of facing a justifiable punishment for various reasons, so instead of endangering herself by telling the truth she will lie to escape her fate. Also BM may actually be so delusional that she believes her lies are true, and tries to convince others of this. This disorder is associated with ADHD and bipolar disorder.

Schizophrenia

Schizophrenia, a chronic brain disorder, affects about two million Americans today. This disease hinders a person's thinking process, emotional and mental stability as well as social ease. People with schizophrenia are often withdrawn and fearful of many things.

Symptoms: BM may have hallucinations and illusions. She may have inappropriate reactions to certain events. For instance, BM may begin laughing hysterically at a funeral, where most people are sad. She may also have delusional thinking, believing that she is spied on or conspired against by you and your husband or even by the President of the United States. BM may speak in a monotonous tone, showing a lack of emotional expression. Also BM's thinking abilities will be hindered. Her speech may be incoherent and her ability to converse is impossible as she jumps from one unrelated topic to the next.

Mental Illness and Substance Abuse

Many people are affected by family members who abuse drugs and alcohol. It's very possible that BM may have turned to substance abuse as a way to escape the realities of her life's circumstances. Health reports show that as many as 50 percent of mentally ill Americans have a substance abuse problem. If BM shows signs of a mental disorder, her substance abuse only heightens her negative behavior. In turn you and your husband probably find it difficult to cooperate with BM when it comes to issues relative to the children.

Symptoms of general substance abuse: BM may show changes in her work attendance, more likely she may be absent or late. She may begin to look sloppy and unkempt, sometimes wearing sunglasses at inappropriate times. BM may begin borrowing money from friends, co-workers and family. She may begin associating with known alcoholics or drug addicts.

Alcohol abuse: You'll notice alcohol on BM's breath and her eyes may appear glazed and shiny. BM may be very passive or unusually combative. Her appearance and hygiene upkeep begins to falter. BM may also have unexplained bruises and accidents, and will become gradually more dysfunctional overall.

Drug abuse (stimulants): Upon seeing BM her eyes may show dilated pupils. She has difficulty sitting still with little or no interest in eating nutritiously or maintaining normal sleeping habits. She may frequently have bad breath and a dry nose and mouth. BM may posses drug stimulant paraphernalia like razor blades, mirrors, small bottles of white powder and small spoons.

Multiple Personality Disorder

More recently referred to as Dissociative Identity Disorder, MPD involves a person's dysfunctional identity. Two or more identities control the individual's behavior at separate times. The different traits within the alter identities of the person include speech, mannerisms, gender, thoughts possibly even ethnicity, social or educational status or age. The personalities may dislike or favor another personality, creating allies or enemies within the same person. A person may have as many as 100 different personalities, with the average being about 10.

❖FAMILY CYCLES OF INSANITY

A good way to gauge whether or not BM could possibly be mentally disturbed is by observing her family members. If you know BM's parents, siblings or any other members of her extended family then their behaviors may be signals as to why BM behaves the way she does.

Your husband probably knows a lot about BM's familial background. It's possible that he has already told you some things about her parents and her upbringing. If your husband tells you that BM's mother "wasn't all there" or that her uncles were alcoholics, then it's not far-fetched that BM has been affected by these behaviors.

Consider your own childhood. The way that your parents and other family members behaved had some influence on who you are today. Whether or not these influenced behaviors come from mental or social disorders doesn't matter. The bottom line is that you have been affected, either negatively or positively, by these behaviors you were exposed to. BM's case is no different. If her mother has one foot inside the crazy house then BM may be a chip off the old lady's block. If BM grew up in a home where getting drunk was the norm, then don't be surprised to see an intoxicated BM from time to time.

It's easy to look objectively at BM and feel sorry for her if you know that she had a hard time growing up. Some BMs may have experienced sexual abuse, witnessed domestic violence between their parents or have had to deal with other family members with social and mental disorders. As a fair woman you can only find it within yourself to have some type of empathy if this is the case in your BM's family life. But just because BM experienced an unfortunate childhood, it doesn't mean that she shouldn't be held responsible for her present day behavior.

So if you think that BM could be a product of her family's social or mental flaws then this may help you to understand how you must approach her. If you know that BM is a drug addict then deal with her accordingly. If you know that

BM is a compulsive liar or has a conduct disorder then accept this and deal with her accordingly. By accepting that BM has certain deficiencies you will lower your expectations and learn how to interact with her in a more efficient manner without becoming emotionally exhausted.

Count your blessings if you are a survivor of a less than stellar childhood. Be proud that you learned how to heal yourself and live your best life. Thank your parents for being loving and proactive. BM is an example of what happens to people who are products of negative exposures during childhood, but who don't know how to move on and beyond. The sad part is that your husband's children may be at risk for following the same cycle of social or mental destruction that BM has continued.

❖You're Not Her Savior

If you and your husband know for a fact that BM has been diagnosed with a mental or social disorder or that she is addicted to a dangerous substance then it is not your responsibility to help cure her. The only reason you and your husband should refer BM to a source for help is if you know that the children will be able to live a better life AND if BM is willing to accept her deficiencies. If BM is in denial about her disorders then there's nothing you or your husband can do.

There are hotlines and pamphlets available that beckon people into support groups and into mental and drug clinics for help. Maybe you or your husband want to anonymously mail a list of hotline numbers or information pamphlets to BM and hope she takes advantage of the assistance that is available. If you are having some serious conflict issues with BM already it would not be wise to directly confront her about getting help. You and your husband, should you choose to make this suggestion, should do so very discreetly or as I said before, anonymously.

Other than making a subtle suggestion for BM to get help, don't use up all of your energy trying to make her life better than what she wants it to be. If she has custody of your husband's children and they are in serious danger, then maybe the only other step you and your husband can take is to motion the court to grant you custody of the children. BM is an adult and if only for the sake of her children she must pull herself up by the bootstraps and find help for whatever her ailments may be. Your only job is to keep her insanity out of your home. If you and your husband are kind enough to assist her, then she should consider herself a very lucky woman.

If you see that your husband wants to help BM then you should step back and let him. Her improvements will mean a better life for his children. But if you notice that your husband is overexerting himself for a lost cause then you should have a serious talk with him. Be compassionate about the way he views BM's disorder when you speak to him, but you should make it clear that he must not drain himself if BM refuses to accept his help.

Don't feel guilty if you look within yourself and find that you really don't care about BM's issues. Don't feel guilty if you don't have the desire to help her find a way to heal, either. BM has family and friends. If BM wanted to be friends with you then you wouldn't be reading this book. Chances are that you may have tried to help BM already but she resisted your approach in a very ugly manner. Why should you want to break your back for someone who won't appreciate your assistance? Your priority is your own mental, physical and social health and you don't want to deflate yourself by giving to others who don't want your help.

6

baby's mama smackdown: the violent baby's mama

❖**SHE'S ALWAYS READY TO RUMBLE**

So BM has threatened to beat you to a bloody pulp. Some wives would gladly take on BM's challenge, while some wives will become paranoid about leaving their homes. I'm sure both sets of women would agree that they'd be better off without having to deal with BM's threats or harassment.

You can't control BM's desire to be alone with you in a medieval torture chamber, and it's quite possible you have the same fantasy starring her. But if she makes this desire known and you become truly fearful for your life and for your family's safety then BM has gone too far. You married a man with a past, but you did not marry a life of harassment, physical threats and discomfort. Society may fool you by rationalizing the situation with some comments as, *You knew what you were getting into* or *Well, what do you expect?* These are nonsensical statements and you should not let this kind of thinking fool you into believing that you deserve anyone's abuse.

Sometimes BM will act out because of her emotional attachment to your husband. This is why (as you read in Chapter 2) your husband must make sure that he never sends BM any mixed messages. Your husband must help BM understand that he is married to a woman he respects more than any other woman, with the exception of his other female relatives. If BM thinks that she can convince your husband to disregard your feelings, then she *will* attempt to walk all over you. You and your husband must always put forth a united front so that BM knows that threats or harassment toward either you or your husband will have equally disturbing consequences.

❖WHO IS BM THREATENING OR HARASSING?

If BM is harassing and threatening you, the courts won't consider you for a domestic violence restraining order. Why? Here's a definition of domestic violence:

Domestic Violence

Domestic violence incident is considered an individual who has received deliberate physical injury or is in fear of imminent deliberate physical injury from a current or former spouse or a current or former cohabitant. This includes a homosexual relationship. In addition, a domestic violence incident is considered to be any crime against:

- A married person living with their spouse.

- A married person estranged from their spouse.

- A male and female person in an intimate relationship who are not married to each other and who are cohabiting or had cohabited.

- Individuals of the same sex in an intimate relationship who are cohabiting or had cohabited.

When it comes to your relationship with BM, you don't fall into any of these categories but your husband does. The majority of law enforcement and government officials don't think that violence occurring between new wives, ex-wives or new girlfriends and ex-girlfriends should fall under domestic violence or else be put in a special category. But if BM is harassing your husband he has a shot at getting a domestic restraining order to protect himself and you.

What if the judge scoffs at your husband's request for a restraining order? This happened to my husband, even though he brought the judge police reports of our BM's threats. Why didn't we get our restraining order? The truth is that many courts are biased toward non-custodial fathers to begin with, so if your husband decides to request a restraining order then make sure he consults with a lawyer first before he makes his case. Make sure that BM's threats are documented either on paper or audio. Your husband must know what kind of information he should supply to win his case.

Moving on to a stickier area—when BM has threatened you. What if she has threatened both you and your husband, but your husband was unable to secure a restraining order? If you still feel unsafe and violated then there are actions you can and should take to protect yourself.

It is possible that BM is so audacious that she believes she can get away with threatening or assaulting you. From anticipating prank phone calls to slashed tires to physical fights on the front lawn, you should not have to live in fear of BM's antics. And contrary to popular belief there *are* ways to find relief and refuge from some batty woman who might as well be the female version of Old Dirty Bastard.

❖THE VEHICLES FOR POPULAR THREATS OF A VIOLENT BM

BMs usually begin their declaration of war with a terroristic threat. A terroristic threat occurs if:

- BM threatens to commit any crime of violence with the purpose to terrorize you or in reckless disregard of the risk of causing such terror.

- BM threatens to commit a crime of violence with the purpose to cause evacuation of a building, place of assembly or facility of public transportation or otherwise to cause serious public inconvenience or in reckless disregard of the risk of causing such evacuation or inconvenience.

On the Telephone

It's 10 p.m. and you pick up the phone. You hear BM on the other line. Immediately your stomach knots up and you can feel the bile rising. For the fifth time this week, BM has called your home in a drunken stupor threatening to punch you in the face because you didn't allow her children to watch "Training Day," a rated-R movie.

Those are my kids. You don't tell them what they can and can't do unless you want my fist upside your face, stupid bitch!

Too many wives have received terroristic threats from BM over the telephone without documenting the incident. How can you get BM to stop terrorizing you if you don't show her that you and your husband mean business? Documenting the content, dates and times of BM's threats via telephone is a good way to gather evidence should you decide to take BM to court for harassment.

On the answering machine: If BM is foolish enough to leave a threat on your answering machine then write down what she said in the message and save the message in your phone system. If the message is in a voice mailbox and not a separate answering machine, use a speakerphone to record the message onto a regular or micro-sized cassette. File a police report immediately. You or your husband can decide to go to court for a final judgment on restraining BM's behavior.

Live on the phone: Write down what prompted the conversation, as well as the time and date the call transpired. Try your best to recall the part of the conversation that included the threat and write this down in a format like this:

> **Your name:** Didn't my husband ask you not to call our home at these hours? Please call back tomorrow morning after 8 a.m.
> **BM (use her name):** What? Who do you think you are telling me not to call your house, huh? Don't let me see you in the street! You'll wish you never met me or my children!
> **Your name:** Excuse me? I know you're not threatening me. You're crazy.
> **BM:** You know what, don't leave your house. Tell your husband, too. I got something for both of you.
> *BM hangs up.*

After you write down what happened on the phone, file a police report immediately. If you believe that BM is on her way to your home then you or your husband should let the police know that you and your husband are uncomfortable. Tell them that you want to identify BM and request that they issue BM a warning. You or your husband can decide to go to court for a final judgment on restraining BM's behavior.

Face-to-Face

BM had the guts to tell you to your face that your legs and arms are better off broken. Maybe you're pregnant, and she said something about harming you so that your unborn baby would be affected. Do your best not to participate in a verbal massacre with this woman. You are too sophisticated to roll around on the ground wrestling, pulling and scratching at a woman who needs a shrink more than a shiner.

As bad as you may want to offer BM the greatest beatdown of her life, do not succumb to your temptations. DO NOT GET INTO A FIGHT WITH BM. If your husband is with you, then both of you need to leave the area right away. If you are alone, avoid saying anything that would add fuel to the fire and leave the area quickly. Take note of the people who witnessed BM threaten you and consider asking them to confirm this when you contact the police.

When you leave, go to a phone booth or use your cellular phone to call the neighborhood police department.

- Tell them that you want to file a police report for a terroristic threat

- Tell them that you are willing to identify BM, and request that they issue BM , a warning

You or your husband can decide to go to court for a final judgment on restraining BM's behavior.

In Writing

Now if BM has e-mailed or snail mailed you terroristic threats then she is making it that much easier for the courts to prosecute her on your behalf.

- Save the letter or print out the e-mail immediately.

- Contact your local police department and file a report.

- Tell them that you are willing to identify BM, and request that they issue BM a warning

You or your husband can decide to go to court for a final judgment on restraining BM's behavior.

❖LET PEOPLE KNOW YOU ARE BEING HARASSED

As embarrassing as Baby's Mama Drama is, you nor your husband should bear the burden of keeping BM's threats a secret. Tell your family members, tell your local police department, ask the mayor and the city council what they can do to further protect your family.

Ask your neighbors to watch out for any suspicious vehicles or people hanging around in front of your apartment building or home. Give anyone you think should be aware a description of BM. Show them a photo, tell them what her car looks like, let them know where she works.

This free-flowing information may entertain some people whom you confide in, but try to focus beyond that. The object is making your community aware that someone wants to physically harm you. If some of your family members look at your dilemma as a juicy piece of gossip, then I'm sure they'll be even quicker to call the police if they see any sign of BM creeping around your neighborhood or your home.

❖ABOUT DOCUMENTING HARASSMENT

I recall one time that BM came to my home unannounced. In fact, it was when my husband and I were dating at the time. I had never even given BM my address! This only led me to believe that she had been spying on us or used some other freakish means to dabble in my business. Let Barnum and Bailey run the circus business because I refuse to have some BM clown knocking at my door. Not only is it rude, but it's downright annoying as hell trying to keep your cool and remained poised. Ghetto spies creeping out the woodwork. It was like I was in Rockwell's "Somebody's Watching Me" video!

I ended up sending BM a very serious declaration (had it notarized, too) of my desire for her to NEVER, EVER set foot upon my premises again without receiving written or verbal permission from me. At the time it felt good to send this letter so that BM could understand that I meant business. But what I did not do was file my complaint with the local police department—so other than my letter I didn't have much municipal backup to tote.

If you do decide to write BM requesting that she stay away from your home, then it's totally understandable. If you and your husband think BM is too unstable to be near your home and the courts won't grant your husband a restraining order then what else are you supposed to do? You're supposed to protect yourself and your family. When you write BM asking her to stay away from your premises:

- In the opening paragraph state your point clearly, i.e., "My husband and I are formally requesting that you no longer come to our home." Do not write an emotionally charged soliloquy.

- In the next paragraph state the most recent incident that has caused you to ban BM from arriving unannounced to your home.

- Clearly list the conditions upon which BM is allowed to come to your home.

- End the letter with your name printed and sign your initials next to your name.

- Give a copy of the letter to your local police department when you file your report. Inform your local city council member and ask him or her for any extra help in keeping BM away. Ultimately if BM violates your request you will have to go to court and request that a judge order BM to stay away from your home.

In a perfect world all wives could safely interact with BM. It would benefit your husband's children the most if they could witness the adults in their lives connecting on a static-free basis. But if you've done your part then you've no reason to feel guilty about protecting yourself and your family. BM must learn that in order to be a part of your life she must play by the rules you and your husband set.

Now don't be surprised if BM receives your letter and then tries to make it appear as if YOU are the harasser. Some BMs will truly try to present their case as if you just decided to send her unsolicited or unwarranted letters asking her to stay away from your home. That is why it is very important for you to state clearly in your letter WHY she has been banned from your property.

Here is an example of a letter.

(BM's Address)
666 Off The Hook Lane
Pointless, NJ 12345

August 4, 2003

Dear <u>(insert BM's name)</u> :

You must receive written or verbal permission from either me or my husband before visiting our home at <u>(your address)</u>.

On August 1 you came to our home and attempted to engage me in a verbal altercation. You used profane language in the presence of the children and caused an ugly and embarrassing scene. My husband and I will not tolerate this behavior from you.

In the future you may only approach our premises in case of an emergency and with our permission. Any violation of our request will lead us to motion our local court to have you prosecuted by the township of <u>(list your town or city)</u>.

Respectfully,

Your Name (you initial here)
Your Husband's Name (your husband initials here)

CC: Your lawyer
(Anyone else that you think should be informed of this matter.)

❖WHEN BM ASSAULTS YOU

In order to identify BM's actions as assault you'll need to know the definitions of two terms that many people get mixed up. Those terms are **simple assault** and **aggravated assault**.

Simple assault occurs if someone intentionally hits you with their hands or shoves you. It's not a life-threatening or maiming act of aggression. This kind of assault falls into the category where there is no dangerous weapon involved and there is no serious injury sustained by the victim. So if BM comes up to you and shoves you, then you can press charges against her for simple assault.

Aggravated assault happens when someone unlawfully attacks you with a weapon with the intention of inflicting severe bodily injury. If BM throws a bottle of lye or bleach in your face, then that would be considered aggravated assault. Any kind of attack involving guns, two-by-four wooden sticks, machetes, bricks, knives and other objects that can be manipulated to seriously hurt someone would fall under the aggravated assault category.

❖IF YOU WANT TO PRESS CHARGES

If BM attacks you, then you should file charges and your husband should support this decision. Your first step is to file a compliant with your police department. After this you would go to your city's court clerk and inform the clerk that you wish to press charges. In the meantime, motion the courts to order BM to stay away from you, your property and your place of employment. Have a copy of your police report with you when you go to the city's court clerk's office.

It is not wise to delay pressing charges if BM has assaulted you. If you take her assault lightly then this sends a message to her that physical conflict is but a mere inconvenience she can inflict upon you at any time. It is not a light matter when someone tries to harm you! It is a violation of your personal space and of your body.

Maybe BM is a woman who grew up scrapping it out in the streets. A scratched face, a bloody mouth or broken bones may be a normal form of communication for BM, but it doesn't have to be a part of your life. File your charges after you have made your complaint with the police. Don't you dare feel for one moment that you are doing something wrong.

You may feel some anxiety about the outcome of pressing charges after BM has attacked you. Some questions racing through your mind might be: *What if BM goes to jail for attacking me? Will my husband be upset at me for putting his chil-*

dren's mother in jail? Who will feed, clothe and bathe the children if BM goes to jail? Will the state take away my husband's children? I hope these answers help calm your nerves.

What if BM goes to jail for attacking me?

If BM is convicted and goes to jail for attacking you then this means that she will have a criminal history. This is what happens when people act like criminals. You shouldn't feel sorry for her or regret making your decision. If BM wasn't connected to your husband and she attacked you, you wouldn't hesitate to sic the police or courts on her, would you? If BM goes to jail and you are afraid that she will try to harm you when she is released then express this to your lawyer, who will take the proper measures to ensure you and your husband will be protected.

Will my husband be upset at me for putting his children's mother in jail?

The only thing your husband has to be upset about is that someone attacked his wife. He should want the savage creature behind bars, too.

Who will feed, clothe and bathe the children if BM goes to jail?

Your husband and the children's extended family can see to it that they are well cared for. If the children have a trusted, nearby relative who is willing to help care for them while their mother is incarcerated, then this is an option your husband may pursue. This way the children are not yanked out of their environment or schools. Your husband can still continue or even increase his visitation.

If your husband would rather have the children live with the both of you during their mother's incarceration then you will have to discuss this decision in detail. Will BM be allowed to call your home collect to speak to her children, or will your husband make other arrangements for their communication? If your husband can have the children move in with the both of you, then you may want to try to warm up to the idea. The children will already be traumatized from seeing their mother off to jail and could use the benefits of having their father with them full time. If you know that your stepchildren are willing to respect your household and do their best to follow your rules, then you really should welcome them into your home. Your good deeds will boomerang back to you in the end.

Will the state take away my husband's children?

If your husband wasn't a loving and responsible father then yes, your state's division of child welfare may pursue making them wards of the state. But since your husband has a history of parental involvement with your stepchildren then he really has nothing to worry about.

❖WHEN BM DAMAGES YOUR PROPERTY

How many wives and their husbands have walked out of their homes only to see the family car's tires slashed? Maybe BM has spray-painted obscenities on the side of your home or vandalized another prized possession of yours. Here's what to do:

File a police report. Call the police department immediately and have them make a report of the time and date you or your spouse discovered your damaged property. Let the police know of any recent threats (which you should have documented and filed anyway) that BM has made toward you.

Take photos of the damaged item(s) right away. If you don't have a camera, then buy one of the drugstore cameras that come with a flash. Take photos of the item the same day you discover it has been damaged.

Take photos of the damaged item from as many angles as possible. Don't just take a photo of your vandalized property from one angle. Take photos from side, back, front and even underneath angles if possible. Take photos of the damaged item up close as well as from a distance. Don't lose the negatives.

Assess the monetary amount of damage. Provide the police with the monetary amount of your damaged property if you can. If you need to have an assessment done by a professional in the case of car damage or vandalism on your home, then provide them with this information at a later date.

File a suit against BM for the amount of money it will cost you to repair the damages, plus any other costs you may have incurred because of her violation of your property. After you have collected all of the information you need to file a suit against BM, then do not hesitate to go to contact a lawyer and move forward with your case. Should you decide to go pro se, meaning represent yourself in court, then at least do your research and consult with a lawyer before making your court appearance.

You aren't the first or the last person who has been violated in someway by an uncivilized person. BM doesn't deserve your patience or your understanding if she tries to hurt you. Please empower yourself, and with your husband's assistance, take the measures necessary to protect yourselves and bring BM to justice.

7

his children, her children

❖**Yup, They're Your Husband's Children**

You love your husband. You love the way he walks, the way he smells, your intimate conversations. You knew he had children when you met him and decided to spend the rest of your life with him, right? So why is it that you sometimes find it difficult to accept his children? It can be hard to accept that your husband fathered children with an incorrigible BM. But it's true and the sooner you emotionally accept this fact, the easier it will be for your prejudices to subside.

Hopefully BM hasn't interfered with your husband's visitation rights. It especially clarifies your perception of the father/children relationship when you are able to spend time with both parties and witness each in their proper roles on a regular basis. The more you see your husband and his children together, the more you will realize what a meaningful relationship they have. This will help you learn how to respect and revere their husband's relationship with his children outside of your marriage.

Unfortunately, if your husband is unable to see his children on a regular basis, then it will be more difficult for you to comprehend a relationship that you hardly ever witness. A marriage is like a town or a village. It has its own culture, its own rules and history. If his children with BM are not a part of your marriage experience you will begin to think of them as temporary guests or even ghosts of his past.

It helps to understand how much your husband loves his young daughter if you see him giving her bubble bath at your home or if you all eat a special dinner together. You'll understand that your husband's son *really is his son* when you see them working on a school project together or if your husband gives him driving lessons on a Saturday afternoon. The children may not live with you and your husband, but if BM encourages a healthy relationship between her children and their father and you, everyone will benefit.

What if your husband isn't able to spend ample time with his children due to friction with BM? What if BM decides that YOU are the reason she will not allow her children to see their father comfortably? If this is the case then your husband should not expect you to cuddle up to or be totally unreserved with children or teenagers whom you barely know. The children need to get used to spending time and space with you. It will be especially difficult for them if they know that BM can't stand you.

You and your husband must discuss ways to make everyone feel more comfortable when his children visit. It is totally normal in some situations for a wife to become disengaged and look upon her stepchildren as "those children." It's normal for you to feel this way and you shouldn't feel guilty about it. Don't you know that some stepchildren disengage themselves from their stepmothers, too? In the beginning, before they get a chance to know what a wonderful person you are, they may think of you as "that lady." Everyone needs time to warm up to each other—stepmothers included.

You didn't give birth to your stepchildren and society shouldn't expect you to become an instant surrogate mother toward them. Besides, your stepchildren would probably feel very smothered and annoyed if you attempted such a thing.

The behavior of the children may further support your indifference to their relationship with your husband. If your husband is a total gentleman, but BM has influenced the children to be boisterous and unmannerly, it will be hard to connect the dots. If the children aren't respectful toward your husband or you or if they just don't call or visit your home often, it isn't hard to fade them into the background of your mind. How are you supposed to seriously respect or even care about their attachment to your husband? Out of sight, out of mind, you may think. Well, that's not the best solution and here's why.

These children, as I hope you did, have a right to know and enjoy their parents. Your husband has taken responsibility for them as their biological father and most likely wants to be a special part in their lives. Try to imagine if you had children, but the law mandated that they had to be raised by a man who was an embarrassment to your past discretions? Wouldn't you want to at least have a small amount of influence on their lives? Your husband wants to be a positive part of his children's lives. Let him.

❖IS YOUR HUSBAND REALLY THEIR DADDY?

What if the child or children don't even look like your husband? You may be tempted to fantasize about one or even all of the children not being biologically related to your husband. Maybe his daughters look nothing like him, maybe they look like BM's family. That's no reason to count them out as not belonging to your husband. Some children may strongly resemble one parent and not the other. Maybe your husband's son is a different complexion, has a different hair color or isn't nearly as handsome as your husband. Between the genes from your husband's side of the family and BM's side of the family, who knows how the children ended up with certain features? You must take science and genetics into consideration here.

If you believe that your husband is acting as father to a child who isn't biologically his then surely you must have thought this before you married him. But maybe you never really wanted to bring up the subject as you knew it might upset your husband. By marrying your husband you made an unspoken agreement to accept the children that he claims. Nevertheless it doesn't guarantee that your discomfort or suspicions will dissolve.

Choose wisely whether or not you want to share your opinions with your husband. You may end up appearing to be heartless and cruel, even if your intentions are innocent. Of course no woman wants her husband unnecessarily dealing with a crazy BM on behalf of a child that isn't even his. It isn't that you're heartless, it's just that it isn't your job to tolerate a BM in your life if the child is not your husband's. It may sound harsh, but you have the right to feel this way.

This is a sensitive area and if you are that uncomfortable with your thoughts then you should speak with your husband. Upon hearing your opinion, he may get offended or he may empathize with your feelings. Ultimately it is your husband's decision whether or not he should seek DNA testing. Also you must decide if you will ultimately accept his children as being biologically his (most likely they are), or if you can live with the fact that you don't believe they (or one of them) are his offspring. Choose this battle wisely.

There are pros and cons to DNA testing. If your husband takes a DNA test and finds out that the child or children are not his, this doesn't mean in all cases that he will be exempt from paying child support. If this happens, you and your husband, depending on the state you reside in should be prepared for a lengthy, expensive court battle. Also think about the effect on the child who must now accept that the person he or she knew to be as her biological "Dad" really isn't. In extreme cases your husband may not want to have anything to do with this child or children if he finds out that they are not his.

If your husband learns that he is not the father of any of his children with BM, feelings of anger, guilt, gullibility, fear and confusion will really take a toll on your marriage. This kind of discovery is a horrible and very irresponsible outcome of a BM's deceit. All parties must accept the consequences and decisions they will have to make if a DNA test is negative.

Should your husband decide to take a DNA test and the results are positive, he will sleep easier knowing that you are both tolerating BM for the sake of the children. It helps to know that the children who receive your husband's child support are actually the rightful recipients. Your husband's money should be spent on the things in his life only for which he is responsible.

Maybe you've never even see a picture of your husband holding his children when they were babies. Maybe his relationship with BM was so unorthodox that the concept of them having children together is beyond your imagination. Don't torture yourself trying to overanalyze and understand the past. They are his children and even though BM is a difficult person it won't change your stepchildren's legal rights or what's on their birth certificates.

- You don't have to accept them as your children, your friends or even refer to them as your stepchildren. You must, however, accept that they are your husband's children.

- It is harder for a wife to acknowledge her husband's relationship with children outside of the marriage if she hardly sees her husband interacting with them.

- If the children are not a part of your everyday life, that doesn't change the fact that they are still your husband's.

- All children may not look like their fathers. This doesn't mean they are not biologically related.

- Think very carefully before suggesting to your husband that he should get a DNA test. This area is a very sensitive one, and a DNA test could open a can of worms. On the other hand it may put BM out of your lives for good.

- The children have a mother and they have a father. Just because they don't live with your husband and you doesn't mean they don't yearn for the love that any child would want from a parent. Don't try to deny them this bond with your husband out of spite toward BM.

Try to accept the children. Try to believe that his children, as separate human beings from BM, will have a positive effect on your husband's emotions and will bring joy to his life. If you are going to be a good wife eventually you will have to believe that they are worthy of your husband's love and his fatherly duties.

❖SHOW YOUR STEPCHILDREN COMPASSION

Many wives are always advised to try to understand their stepchildren's pain. But while you and your husband experience your own battle with BM's threats and erratic behavior, who is there to understand your pain? It's hard enough learning how to eliminate the harm that BM may try to cause you. It can seem like an emotional burden if you try to set aside understanding for the children. In your disgust you may even think, *If it weren't for them* (meaning the children) *I'd never have to deal with BM!*

It's true that if the children were never conceived, BM wouldn't be a part of your life. But do you think that the children, while in her womb, were even aware of what the future would hold? Do you think that the children played a big factor in deciding that their mother would be a lunatic or an emotionally unstable person? Many children, who live with what **you** consider to be a crazy BM, actually love their mother unconditionally. Even if BM tells them terrible things about your husband and you their loyalty will remain with her. So don't hold it against them if they were born to a person like BM. It wasn't their choice.

Just as the children didn't choose to be born to two estranged parents, you didn't give their mother an invitation to swing from the trees in your backyard like some deranged monkey. It is not your fault that your husband decided to spend the rest of his life with you and not BM. You need not feel apologetic or guilty about their broken family. You don't owe the children an apology for your happiness. So then what kind of compassion *should* you show the children?

Anyone should be compassionate toward any child with a foul-mouthed, violent and unmotivated parent. Think about all of the adjectives that describe BM. Imagine you were a social worker or a teacher and that these children were your students. Wouldn't you feel sad that these students were exposed to such negative energy on a constant basis? Your husband's children with BM must endure all of her characteristics. Many times they are too afraid to critique their mother's behavior for fear that she will lash out at them, too. The children's minds and innocence are poisoned for the sake of BM's selfishness. This alone is a tragedy.

Dr. Judith Wallerstein, a prominent researcher of divorce and its impact on children in the U.S., has some interesting findings on what your stepchildren may be going through. Her studies show that divorced or single parents provide less time, less discipline and are less sensitive toward their children as they are caught up in their own emotional healing or demise. Parenting is put on the backburner and the quality of childrearing diminishes.

But it isn't your job to save them from BM. All of us have burdens to bear in life and your husband's children will have their challenges to face with their mother, just as you may have had to with your parents. Unless BM is illegally harming the children, it isn't worth your time to attempt morphing into their Saving Grace—especially if you aren't genuinely inclined to do so.

Your husband is a good father. If you and your husband have children of your own, then you'll really see what his children with BM are missing out on. They can't sit on his lap while watching the Saturday night scary movie. They can't always ask him to draw a diagram that will help them with their math homework. When they have nightmares, your husband is not usually the person who runs to their room to calm and comfort them.

BM is usually the one who deals with their nightmares, helps them with homework or decides what movies they will watch. These children will not have the everyday wisdom and love from your husband. Whatever BM's talents, cultural exposure and personality entails, this is what the children will get 90 percent of the time. If BM refuses to learn how to speak standard English, don't be surprised if the children follow suit. If BM likes to drink and party all of the time, the children will be left to entertain themselves. If BM puts low expectations on their behaviors, the children will lack self-respect and self-discipline.

❖How BM Shortchanges Your Husband's Son

It isn't your stepson's fault or your fault that his father doesn't live with him, but he *would* benefit from having his Dad in his life more often. A smart BM wouldn't let her anger or jealousy cheat her son out of a healthy relationship with his father. Yet many sons have to witness hearing their mothers endlessly insult their fathers.

A boy may eventually feel as if his mother is insulting a part of him, too. His self-esteem is lowered and he may end up suppressing resentment toward BM, while trying to make his own assessment of his father's personality. In the worst case, a boy may even side with his mother and shun his father based on her lies. The boy loses out on a potential bond with his father and may have to settle for dealing with his mother's boyfriends or a stepfather. Not that these other men in the boy's life are meaningless, but his right to know his father is primary and should be honored.

Some BMs have an emotionally unhealthy attachment to their sons. In a sick BM's mind she wants her son's love to replace the love that she feels his father never gave her. This kind of behavior is known as emotional incest. You can read more about it in Patricia Love's book *Emotional Incest Syndrome*. In this instance a parent "dumps" all of his or her adult feelings and needs onto their child, and forces the child to play the role of comforter and soother. BM begins to believe that her son or "little man" is really capable of making her feel loved, beautiful and attractive in the way that a grown man could. How can an adult woman want to be validated romantically by her own son? The movie character Norman Bates of "Psycho" is a prime example. His mother had a bizarre attraction toward him, yet at the same time repulsion for him based on the fact that Norman could never become his father. A BM such as this can be very damaging to her son's ability to adjust socially as a child, teenager and adult.

There are also BMs who will not discipline their sons appropriately for fear of looking like the bad or mean parent. BM may even saturate him with her own ignorant philosophies, humor and morals to purposely stunt his intellectual growth. You may notice that everything your stepson says or does is a reflection of BM's thinking. This kind of BM allows her son to underachieve in everything he does, since pushing him to be his best would be sharpening his potential. That is, his potential to grow and become an individual with his own ideas.

Although it is normal for a son to have a strong affection for his mother it's abnormal for a boy to become mentally and emotionally handicapped as a result of this "love." This is not love that BM is showering her son with; it is her fear, her rage and her selfishness. It is her need to be validated through the control of her child's emotions. Instead of BM learning how to heal her own pain with the help of a therapist, her son becomes her romantic and emotional crutch—her "little" man. Sickening, huh?

If BM continues to skimp on disciplining her son in various areas, we all know that the general society won't have the same level of tolerance. The wake-up calls will be harsh and unforgiving for BM's son as he gets older. If your husband were welcomed as a healthy part of his son's life, surely some of BM's harmful effects might be tapered.

❖BM's Insecurities Hurt Her Daughter

As for girls, not having reasonable time with their fathers can have even more devastating effects than a boy who is estranged from his father. BM is the primary example of womanhood and motherhood for her daughter. BM's daughter will emulate many of her mannerisms, opinions and her likes and dislikes. If BM is too busy trying to impress her new boyfriend, her daughter will learn that it is okay to have children and then ignore them for sexual pleasure. If BM has a habit of sucking her teeth, or rolling her eyes as a form of communication, her daughter may begin to imitate these behaviors as early as 3-years-old.

Some BMs are especially afraid that if their daughters form a special bond with you, the stepmother, that their daughters will no longer be impressed with them. A confident BM already understands that her bond with her daughter is an unbreakable and everlasting one. But a BM who is insecure will have serious issues with you spending time around her little girl or teenager.

Maybe you and your husband have exposed his daughter to new experiences. She may tell BM about all of the fun she has when she is with you and her father. A typically irrational BM becomes threatened if you cooked a new, different meal for her daughter, showed her how to speak a new language or bought her a new book. BM doesn't realize that you don't have to entertain anyone's child except your own, yet she is ungrateful for your kindness toward her child. BM translates your tenderness as your plot to take her place. Instead of BM being happy that you are willing to make her child comfortable in your home and with your husband, she looks upon you as some desperate kidnapper.

If BM has a tendency to allow men to go in and out of her life then this is an indicator that she validates herself through the approval of men, even if that approval is sexually motivated. Imagine how this practice may trickle down to her daughter. Her daughter may become obsessed with having boyfriends at an early age, especially if BM shares graphic information about her sexual affairs with her daughter. Also if BM does not know her partners very well, or chooses to marry a man out of convenience this can put her daughter and her son in danger of being sexually molested, physically or emotionally abused. These consequences may sound extreme but they do happen.

Daughters should be comfortable in seeking their fathers for advice, protection and love. Some BMs agree with this notion and are willing to allow your husband time with his daughter only if YOU are not present. If you try to influence or grow to love BM's daughter, it only makes you look like a caring and loving woman. BM wants to believe with all her heart that you are evil with ill intentions. By denying that you are as beautiful and kind as you really are, BM copes with her own shortcomings and lack of confidence in her mothering skills.

Girls are very affected by the relationships they have with their fathers. They will learn how to set their standards in dealing with men. They will learn that they have the right to be protected and that men, in general can be kind and friendly. If BM's daughter is exposed to the wrong type of male role models, this could affect her for the rest of her life. Many girls who don't have a substantial relationship with their fathers end up on a lifelong quest to find a father's love—but in all the wrong places. The only place BM's daughter will ever know a true father's love is from your husband.

Stepmothers must sometimes step up to the plate when BM has failed. There is no task of parenting that a stepmother somewhere hasn't done on behalf of a BM. Sometimes wives must wash the dirty hair of BM's children. Some women must clean underneath their stepchildren's fingernails or teach them how to use "thank you" and "please" on a regular basis. You may have had to take your husband's daughter to the museum or library for term paper research. Maybe you had to have a long talk with your husband's teenage son about hygiene. These children may get the basics from BM, but sometimes they are also missing out on a lot. Don't expect BM to ever thank you for giving her a helping hand with her children.

Your husband is the only person that is obligated to give 100 percent of himself, as it is his child. Many wives do these extra deeds out of kindness, because it is certainly not their responsibility to cater to the child if he or she lives with BM. You and your husband know that the quality of life the children have with BM might not be the best, but given the chance, you both do what you can emotionally and financially to enrich the children's lives. It is sad that BM punishes your husband for being happy with you by shortchanging the lives of their children.

Here are some tips on staying compassionate toward the children.

- It isn't your fault that the children's father doesn't live with them. It is up to the BM to learn how to co-parent properly for the sake of her children.

- The children did not choose to have an ignorant mother. It is not their fault that she was their first teacher.

- The children are missing out on the day-to-day perks of living with a caring, fun and responsible father.

- The children are probably being exposed to an atmosphere that is below the standard of your husband's and your choice.

- Sometimes the children are being used as BM's emotional crutches, romantic fill-ins and pawns.

- The children won't be able to shape the quality of their lives until they are brave enough to stand up to their mother, if they ever mentally develop that far to see through her lies.

- BM may put her own marriage or romantic life before her children.

- For boys, BM may be stripping them of the right to have a good male role model and loving parent.

- For girls, BM is the role model and is probably too insecure to give her daughter the freedom to enjoy being with you.

- Your stepchildren may not be as close to your husband as the biological children between you and your husband will be. This is not anything to be apologetic for, but just a fact to help you see things from your stepchildren's side of the fence.

The children are being deprived, fooled or neglected by BM on some level. This is where your compassion comes in. When the children are rude, remember that this is a reflection of the atmosphere that BM provides for her children. When the children appear to be ignorant of things that other children their age should know or understand, remember that BM was their first teacher. Be compassionate about these children not having full contact with their father or you. You are a special person and they are very, very fortunate that you choose to be kind and gracious toward them. BM tries to block her children's blessings constantly, and her selfishness doesn't even allow her to care.

❖WHEN THEY TALK ABOUT "MOMMY"

Although BM probably isn't a pleasant topic of discussion in your home, this will change when your stepchildren visit. BM may be the last thing you want to hear about, even if it's from her own children. You don't have to sit and listen to the children's constant praise of a BM that you know is verifiably insane but you will have to learn how to control your facial expressions (you know that face I'm talking about) and your verbal responses (*I really don't feel like hearing about your crazy mother*). There are ways to stay respectful when the children speak about BM, and there are ways to keep the torture to a minimum.

First you must understand that it doesn't matter if a child is 7 or 17, chances are they love their mother. They shouldn't have to view BM in the same light that you and your husband see her. You and your husband know she's not a nice person. The children, however, have a different experience. Trust me, BM is probably a lot nicer to her children than she is to you and your husband. Does that mean she isn't abusive or neglectful of the children? Of course not. It just means that the relationship is different and once you accept that the children will love BM unconditionally then you'll understand why they speak about her—even in your home.

My mommy has that CD. My mommy said that Kevin (BM's boyfriend) messed her hair up in the shower. Why don't you fry your chicken instead? That's what my mother does. My mother usually takes me out shopping whenever I want. My mother drinks beer and she let me taste it before. Wanna see how my mother dances?

There will be a host of things that children, young and teenaged, will disclose about their mother. They will say things in praise of their mother. They will also say things that only serve to confirm why you are disgusted with BM's behavior. How do you deal with either one?

Never tell the children that they are forbidden to speak about their mother in your home. In addition, never tell your husband that the children should be prohibited from speaking about their mother. You and your husband want the children to be comfortable in your home. The children should be able to freely express their emotions no matter where they are. It is beneficial to them and as adults you should not hinder this important part of their development.

In BM's house she may tell the children not to ever mention your name or even your husband's. BM may tell the children to keep secrets about what is going on in her home. If the children are on the verge of being homeless, or if BM's boyfriend gets drunk on a regular basis BM may drill it into her children's minds that they must absolutely keep her business private (*Don't ya'll be going over there telling all my business!*). This kind of information is just what you and your husband need to know. If you silence the children, they may never feel comfortable enough to divulge important information regarding life at home with BM. It really is best to let the children know that they are free to say whatever they really feel when they are with you and your husband.

So how will you overcome having to listen to tales of BM's great cooking? How will you avoid vomiting or cruelly laughing when your stepdaughter shows you how BM dances? You must remember that in these children's eyes, BM is the only mother they've been "blessed" to know. She is a cornerstone in their lives so it's normal for them to speak about her often. In their world they eat, sleep and breathe BM.

Here are some examples on how to respond when the children make positive comments about BM:

> **CHILD:** My mommy cooks the best dinner.
> **YOU:** That's really nice.
>
> **CHILD:** My mother's handwriting is so pretty.
> **YOU:** That's wonderful.
>
> **CHILD:** When my mom gets her nails done, she lets me get mine done, too.
> **YOU:** That's great.

Keep your responses short and sweet. Many times wives, and even their husbands, are tempted to prod BM's children for more information. Wives and their husbands who deal with Baby Mama's Drama want to make sure that the children in BM's custody are safe and are in a decent atmosphere. This is one reason why you or your husband may encourage a child to give you more detail on life with BM. It isn't necessary to beat around the bush if you are truly concerned about the child's welfare. Don't play mind games with the child so that you can get information. If your husband is on speaking terms with BM he can ask her important questions himself.

Sometimes it isn't harmful to ask the child general questions out of concern. But you must be very tactful in deciding which questions are appropriate and which ones should be dealt with through the adults.

Here's an example of how to make sure that you don't put the child in an awkward position:

> **CHILD:** We had Burger King for dinner last night. We always have Burger King.
> **WIFE:** Oh, that's nice. Does your mommy cook vegetables for you sometimes?
> **CHILD:** Yes.
> **WIFE:** Good. What are your favorite vegetables?
> **CHILD:** Spinach and sweet peas.

In this conversation the wife is able to find out if the child is being fed vegetables at BM's home. The wife doesn't insult BM's affinity for hamburgers and french fries. At the same time the wife is also able to find out what her stepchild's favorite vegetables are. This kind of harmless conversation touched on BM, but the wife steered it into a productive direction.

Here's an example of how the same conversation could have taken a nasty turn:

> **CHILD:** We had Burger King for dinner last night. We always have Burger King.
> **WIFE:** Oh really? Does your mother ever cook you real food?
> **CHILD:** Yes. We eat White Castle, too.
> **WIFE:** That's not real food! Good grief, she doesn't even feed you any vegetables? She probably gives you Kool-Aid and cheese doodles for breakfast.
> *Child is silent.*

The wife in this conversation allowed her feelings about BM to make the child feel uncomfortable. This isn't fair. Although the wife may be extremely disgusted with BM's nutritional values, there are other ways to help the child remember to eat vegetables or healthier foods. The wife in this conversation accomplished nothing by insulting BM in front of the child. The wife could have discussed her findings with her husband and they both could have decided how to deal with the way BM feeds the child. She didn't even appreciate that her stepchild was comfortable enough to speak freely. Many stepchildren are hesitant to discuss BM comfortably in their father and stepmother's home.

When your stepchildren decide to volunteer information about BM, act as if you are having any other normal conversation. Don't whip out a notebook pad and a micro-cassette recorder. Don't make the child feel as if he or she is on a witness stand at a trial. The more relaxed you are the more the child will get to know you and be comfortable in expressing his or her thoughts.

❖KEEPING SECRETS

You and your husband must make your stepchildren understand that there are some secrets that shouldn't be kept. If drug, emotional or sexual abuse is taking place in BM's home, your stepchildren should know that it's okay to tell you and your husband. Not only is it okay, the children should understand that it is mandatory. Make sure that once they are old enough the children know how to dial your home phone number and that they can reach your husband in case of an emergency.

Here is an example of helping a child understand that she or he needs to talk more about a "secret" they may be holding.

> **CHILD 1:** My mother's boyfriend is always yelling at her.
> **CHILD 2:** Shhhh! Mommy told us not to tell any of her business!
> **WIFE** (to Child 2): It's okay if (Child 1) she feels like she wants to talk about it. You both know that we don't keep those kinds of secrets in this house.
> **WIFE** (to Child 1): Does your mother's boyfriend scare you?
> **CHILD 1:** Yes. He said he would knock my head off and he said that I eat too much.
> **WIFE** (to Child 1): Oh, those are mean things to say. Did that make you upset?

The wife gives the child a chance to express her feelings. If the child has nothing more to say the wife end the conversation, and changes the subject. She should also inform her husband right away so that the child can relate these feelings to her father.

It is important to inform the father immediately upon hearing disturbing information from your stepchildren. It's great if your stepchild is comfortable talking to you, but he or she must be able to speak with their father just as well. If your husband isn't available immediately, use your own discretion as to whether you should continue the conversation.

If the child is more open with you than with your husband use this advantage to get more details about the incident and about the child's feelings. Relay all of this to your husband as soon as you can. If the child is comfortable with speaking to your husband, then it is best to bring the conversation to a close and bring your husband into the room to join in the discussion.

In the conversation example above, Child 2 was reluctant to allow his or her sibling to divulge information out of loyalty to BM. The wife didn't get into a long and drawn out debate with Child 2. That is a waste of energy. As the adult she simply stated the household rules and focused her attention back to Child 1. That's what you need to do should you encounter a similar situation.

❖DON'T BE NOSY

When stepchildren decide to share information about living with BM, sometimes wives can't help but to be nosy. It's almost like live entertainment. You get to have a front row seat in the life of a curious creature, not unlike a show from The Animal Planet channel. It's tempting isn't it? But you know you have better things to do with your time than to become an undercover tabloid reporter or biographer on the life of BM.

Here's an example of just how nosy some wives can be:

> **WIFE:** So, is your mother working today?
> **CHILD:** No. She went to get her hair done because she's going to a party tonight.
> **WIFE:** What kind of party? Who's having a party?
> **CHILD:** I don't know.
> **WIFE:** Have you ever seen her get dressed for a party?
> **CHILD:** Yes.
> **WIFE:** Wow, that must be interesting. What kind of clothes does she wear? Short skirts with a lot of red lipstick?
> **CHILD:** Yes. She likes to wear her favorite blonde wig a lot.
> **WIFE:** What time does she come home? Pretty late, I bet.
> **CHILD:** Sometimes we don't see her until the next day. My grandmother says my mother needs to grow up and stop spending all her money on clothes because we don't even have a lot of books to read at home. She just buys herself magazines.
> **WIFE:** That's a shame.

More than likely this wife already knew that BM neglected her children on some level. The only reason she was prodding the child for information was for her own personal satisfaction. It's true everything that the child said confirmed the fact that BM is indeed a loser, but the wife should not have asked the child those questions unless it was absolutely necessary. The wife in this conversation could have lived without the extra details on BM and the child could have lived without the wife's shameless interrogation.

You wouldn't like it if BM asked your stepchild all kinds of personal information about you and your husband. BM probably does this, but that doesn't mean that you should stoop to her level. If she wants to fixate herself on the highs and lows of your life instead of improving her own, that's her problem. You can't help it if you've become the latest celebrity to step out on BM's red carpet, but don't fall into the trap of believing her life is worth picking your stepchild's brain.

❖TALKIN' 'BOUT THE GOOD OLD DAYS

It is difficult to hear your stepchild talk about the time when BM and your husband were together. Your stepchildren have the right to reminisce about their family history, but there is a very thin line of reality and fantasy over which they must not trip. Before you even married your husband, the children should have been made to understand that the romantic relationship between BM and their father was over. I'm not saying that they should be made to believe that their parents were never together, but they shouldn't be taught to obsess upon or hope for the past to return.

Here's an example of a stepchild treading too far down memory lane:

CHILD: You know I used to bring my mother and father cereal in bed.
WIFE: Oh that's nice.
CHILD: They'd both kiss me on the forehead and then they'd start kissing each other over and over and over again.
WIFE: Yes, that's what husbands and wives do. They show affection in many different ways. That's why I love being married to your father. He's got the greatest hugs in the world.
CHILD: He used to hug my mother, too.
WIFE: Oh yes, I know. It's probably strange having to see your father hug a new person. You probably had some good times when your parents were together. Maybe your should talk to your dad about how much you miss him.

Does this wife deserve the Nobel Peace Prize or what? The wife didn't get angry or snappy. At this point the wife should change the subject and make sure that she informs her husband about the awkward conversation. Later on her husband can have a serious talk with his child about his or her feelings.

Sometimes wives can overreact and be very cruel to a child for reminiscing too much. Here's an example:

CHILD: You know when my mother and father were married they danced together all the time.
WIFE: Don't you know that your mother and father aren't married anymore? Why do you think I care what your mother and father did?
CHILD: I don't know.
WIFE: Well, let me tell you something. In my house I don't want to hear anything about your father and your mother dancing, kissing, hugging or anything like that. I'm the wife. Your father does not love your mother. If you want to keep talking about them dancing then I suggest you take your little behind back to your mother's house.
CHILD: I hate this house anyway.
WIFE: Good, I'll ask your father to take you home right now.

Things just got out of control here. Much of it could have been avoided had the wife remained calm. Again, her feelings regarding hearing about BM and her husband are normal, but her reaction does nothing to teach the child or to strengthen her own bond with the child. In the end, the child is pushed back even further into a world of fantasy where she or he expects or wishes that BM and his or her father will reunite.

❖WHEN BM TELLS THEM THINGS ABOUT YOU

What if your stepchildren relay things that BM has said about you or your husband? This isn't easy to handle all the time.

> **CHILD:** My mother said you took my Daddy away from us.
> **WIFE:** Why would she say that?
> **CHILD:** She said that you and my Daddy want us to be poor.
> **WIFE:** I'm really sad that your mother thinks those horrible things about your father and me. But I have to tell you something. Those things aren't true. Your father and I love each other very much and we want the best for you. Do you think we want to see you starve?
> **CHILD:** No.
> **WIFE:** When you visit us, don't we always feed you?
> **CHILD:** Yes.
> **WIFE:** Your father also works very hard to send your mother money so that she can buy you clothes and toys and other things. Your mother buys you clothes and toys, right?
> **CHILD:** Yes.
> **WIFE:** And another thing. Daddies are very special because no one can ever take them away from their children. Your father may not live with you but that doesn't mean he doesn't love you. Do you think I would want your daddy to forget about you? Does your father treat you well and show you how much he loves you?
> **CHILD:** Yes.
> **WIFE:** I don't know why your mother would say that, but you'll never lose your daddy and he'll never let you become poor.
> **CHILD:** Okay.

In this conversation the wife is hit with two accusations. The first is that that she is a Daddy-thief. The second is that she and her husband want to see the children live in poverty. These are two of the most common accusations many wives hear from their stepchildren. This wife is smart and uses the child's own logic to rebut the comments that BM has made to the child. The wife points out to the child what *is* true. The truth is that the child's father loves them and financially supports them. There is no need to continue the conversation after the wife has made her point.

In addition the wife should mention the conversation with her husband. The wife can express her disgust, shock or other emotions about the things that BM has told the child when she talks to her husband. If the wife's husband desires, he may also talk to the child about the things that BM has said.

Some BMs are famous for telling their children that their father's wife or girl-friend has "stolen" or "taken" him away from them. If this has happened to you then please understand that you have no control over BM's perception of why she and your husband broke up. If she wants to fill her children's heads with even more confusion then all you can do is defend yourself if the subject ever comes up. You can't change her way of thinking.

Here is an example of when wives allow their emotions to take over conversations like this:

> **CHILD:** My mother said that you're stupid.
> **WIFE:** Well, let's see. You're mother can hardly speak English properly and couldn't even make it out of community college. If anything, I think your mother's the stupid one. You tell her I said that.
> **CHILD:** Well, my mother's not stupid and she said that you stole my daddy away from me!
> **WIFE:** Maybe if your mother lost a little weight and was a nicer person, your father wouldn't have left her.
> **CHILD:** I'm telling my mother you called her fat.
> **WIFE:** Well, she is.
> *Child storms out of the room.*

The wife had every right to be disturbed by the nasty things BM told the child. No one wants to hear these kinds of things about themselves. The way this wife *feels* is normal, but the way she reacted is not. The wife should have remembered that BM's jealousy and bitterness are constantly transferred to an innocent child. BM has no concept of the damage she does to the child when relaying these negative ideas.

The way that the wife handled the conversation was counter-productive. The child now sides with BM in believing lies about the wife. The wife should have found a more gentle way to deal with the child who was brave enough to share BM's ignorant comments.

Here's what should have happened:

> **CHILD:** My mother said that you're stupid.
> **WIFE:** That's not very nice. Your mother doesn't really know me. Sometimes

people make mistakes and misjudge other people for their own reasons. I know I'm smart. Your dad knows I'm smart and my friends know I'm smart. Didn't I help you with your homework the other day?

CHILD: Yes.

WIFE: Well, that's what smart people like me do—they help smart kids with their homework right?

CHILD: Yes.

WIFE: One more thing. When people say mean things like that, we don't repeat them in this house. If your mother thinks I'm stupid that's fine, but this is my house and your father's house and we don't like hearing things like that here. It doesn't help anyone and it doesn't make anyone feel good to hear it. Did you feel good when your mother said that to you?

CHILD: Not really.

WIFE: Exactly. Let's talk about more intelligent things okay?

CHILD: Okay.

In this conversation the wife takes the focus off of BM and highlights the truth. The truth is that the wife *is* smart and that BM's insults have been disputed, but not in a rude way as to hurt or intimidate the child. The wife also makes it clear that she is not interested in hearing the negative things BM says about her.

It is very important that wives speak to their husbands about disturbing comments that the stepchildren make. Often the husband may not be there at the time the child says certain things to the wife. This can be a very tempting time for a wife to want to knock the child into the next week for repeating BM's insults. As a wife you may want to argue with the child or punish the child for repeating BM's vulgarities and lies. Don't lose yourself to this silly game. BM is using her own child as a vessel for emotional poison. Just hope that the child survives being raised by such a person.

By talking to your husband about how you feel, you will avoid giving the child your own adult feelings about BM. Your stepchild already has one irrational person to deal with, don't double his or her burden. BM's sickness will affect her children and you don't want to add to the damage. Your husband will be able to discuss the children's behavior with them, and if necessary your husband will let BM know that she should not deal with her anger by burdening the children with lies or bitterness toward you, his wife. Maybe you and your husband will decide that BM is not even worthy of trying to change.

Don't forget:

- It is normal for children of all ages to share general information about their mothers.

- When your stepchildren mention their mother in a general way, i.e., "My mother has a car like that one" keep your comments short and sweet.

- Don't unnecessarily prod the children for information about life at home with BM.

- Don't insult BM in front of the children.

- If your stepchild tells you that BM says nasty things about you, try to remember what kind of person BM is so that you're not surprised.

- If your stepchild tells you that BM says nasty things about you, always defend yourself and your husband. Don't focus on BM's lie. Focus on what is true.

- Make sure your stepchildren know what secrets are okay to talk about in your home.

- Don't make the children feel awkward every time they talk about their mother.

- Your husband should explain to the stepchildren that BM's and his romantic history is in the past. There is no need for them to share too much of this information with you, nor should you want them to.

- Learn how to keep your cool so that your future relationship with the stepchild is not threatened by BM's foolish comments.

The most important thing is keeping the peace in your home. If BM chooses to dissolve her own children in an atmosphere of chaos it is out of your husband's and your control once the children return to her home.

❖THE BM COOTIES

You're eating a slice of leftover pizza and your young stepson's eyeing your slice as if it were made from the finest dough and gourmet cheese in all of America. You get a knife and cut him a small piece. There's no way in hell you'd let him bite the same slice of pizza or drink from the same cup of hot chocolate. Not that you have anything against him, you just don't want BM's germs.

It sounds immature, doesn't it? Some wives cringe at the thought of any physical contact with BM's children because they believe that BM's germs, nastiness or bacteria will enter their bloodstream, lungs or mucous membranes. In fact, they'd rather let a child they'd never met before share an ice cream cone with them before ever eating after one of BM's children.

The truth is that these wives know that BM's children eat after their mother, kiss their mother and sit on the same toilet seat as their mother. The wife can even acknowledge that her husband was once intimate with BM, but most likely that physical contact was years before. These children actually touch BM everyday. Use the same shower. A wife may visualize that BM's children are a vessel for the deadly germs of BM and therefore she will do anything to avoid intimacy with the children.

If you suffer from the fear of catching BM Cooties then by all means, don't be so hard on yourself. It's very similar to elementary school students who don't want to touch the boy who looks different or the girl who speaks with a funny accent. The mere thought of BM repulses you. Maybe it's because she actually does look as if she carries some type of reoccurring infection. Maybe it's because her personality is just as nasty. Whatever your reasons, you'd never want to touch her or be close enough that her breath, spit or smell would invade your space or body. And since her children cuddle up to her, you feel that she is indirectly infecting your house with "BM dirt" through the children.

Your stepdaughter may use your comb or brush without permission. If you're afraid of the BM Cooties you'll probably end up throwing away the hair utensils. Your stepson wants to kiss you, but you can't ignore the fact that his lips also kiss that creature who gave birth to him. You tell him that you'd rather a handshake, but even this makes you nauseas.

At some point you do have to grow up. If BM doesn't have some contagious disease then you really should calm down. In the case where BM may have a disease that she could pass on to the children, who could then pass it on to you and your husband—there are ways to overcome your BM-germophobia.

In the bathroom:

- You should decide if you want to share your comb or brush with your stepchildren. Just because they are children doesn't mean that you should let them use your personal items. Maybe you don't even let your friends use your hairbrush. It depends on your personality.

- If you do allow your stepchildren to use your comb or brush, soaking the hair utensils afterward in hot water and a soap solution may make you feel more comfortable. Hygienically, it also makes sense for you to wash your comb and brush if a non-relative uses either one.

- You can't prevent your stepchildren from using your bathroom. They will not transfer any gangrene from BM's derriere by sitting on your toilet. When they are visiting, you may purchase antibacterial wipes and wipe the toilet seat each time before you use it.

- Your stepchildren should not use your toothbrush. Have your husband purchase their own toothbrushes to keep at your house.

- Have disposable cups for mouthwash.

- Make the stepchildren, if they are old enough, clean the bathtub after they shower. You should not have to clean up anybody's shower scum and no one should have to clean up yours. Make sure you leave them a clean bathtub, too. If the children are young, put on rubber cleaning gloves and clean the bathtub after they've used it.

- Make sure they have their own towels and washcloths.

In the kitchen or dining room:

- You don't have to let your stepchildren eat after you if it makes you uncomfortable. Tell them that you will cut them a piece of your sandwich or that you will give them their own cup of ice cream.

- If you are uncomfortable with drinking from the same cup or beverage bottle as your stepchildren, then don't. Allow them to have their own personal access to the juice, soda, water or whatever it is that you are drinking. If you are drinking from a bottle and there is no cup available then drink what you desire first and save the rest for the stepchildren. This way you won't have to drink after them. This will only work if they don't mind drinking after you.

When they want to be affectionate:

If you believe that the affection your stepchildren want to give you is genuine, then it really is best to accept that hug or that kiss. BUT if you aren't ready to, or don't believe that the stepchildren are genuine in their affection then here's how to get around the surface mushiness.

- If you aren't comfortable with hugs from your stepchildren then say that you're not a person that hugs a lot. "Oh, that's okay. You don't have to hug me. I'm not a huggy kind of person." Offer a handshake instead.

- If you don't want to be kissed then offer a light hug instead. Tell the stepchildren that you're not a "kissy kind of person." If you don't want to offer a light hug then offer a handshake instead.

- If you don't want a stepchild to sit on your lap or rest his or her head against your shoulder them offer them a comfortable alternative. Offer a pillow, or a nearby couch or tell them to rest on their father's lap.

- It will take time for you to get used to your husband's children becoming intimate with you, don't rush what you don't feel.

If the child is sick or needs you to help clean him/her up:

- If your husband is unavailable to clean up the child, have a pair of cleaning rubber gloves and a mask handy for cleaning up vomit, urine or feces. Some mothers do this with their own children so you're not being extra sensitive.

- If your stepchild's nose is bleeding or is full of mucous and your husband is not immediately available to assist the child, allow the child to blow his or her own nose if he or she is old enough. If not, use more tissue than usual so that their mucous or blood does not touch your fingers.

- If the child has fallen and scraped a knee, busted a lip, etc. wear latex gloves and use a Q-tip or cotton ball to apply ointment or medication.

- **If the child is extremely hurt** and your husband is not available, then as a responsible adult you don't have to time for being fussy and bothered by the BM Cooties. **Do what is best immediately for the child.**

The younger your stepchildren are, the more they will want to give you sloppy kisses or be closer to you. It may take some wives a while to adjust to their husband's children hugging her or using her toilet. Just because you married your husband doesn't mean you'll become enthusiastic about affection or becoming intimate with his children.

Please do remember that rejection does hurt. If you need to take a while to get used to your stepson's hugs, then take your time. But at least make it a goal to accept his hugs one day.

Don't make your stepchildren feel as if they have the cooties, when it's really their mother who turns your stomach. And if she turns your stomach so much that you risk rejecting simple hugs and signs of affection from your stepchildren then you're wasting too much time internalizing her negativity. It's not the children that are in danger of infecting you, it's your own mind. Try to concentrate on what's positive about the children instead of how much their mother disgusts you.

As for personal items and sharing food, that is entirely up to you. Your husband should not expect you to share combs, toothbrushes or saliva with his children. For some people, drinking and eating after others is an unclean practice. If you do not want to be that intimate you don't have to. Not with your stepchildren, or anyone else.

Eventually you may learn that you like hugging your stepdaughter, or combing her hair. Maybe you might share an ice cream soda with your stepson and then allow him to kiss you on the cheek afterward. As you get to know your stepchildren they will become more individual to you in contrast to mini-versions of BM. You will begin to credit your stepchildren with their own characteristics and personas instead of equating them so closely with BM's behavior.

You should also make sure that you gently explain these feelings to your husband. Tell him that you need time to allow your stepchildren to get physically close to you. You can even tell him that you don't want BM's germs to get on you. As crazy as it sounds he may humor you and give you your space to adapt. He knows that his children shouldn't be forced to receive hugs and kisses from you. Your husband knows that his children shouldn't have to drink from the same glass of milk as you if they don't want to. He shouldn't have a problem understanding your point of view.

As long as you make sure to be tactful and not offensive to the children, there's nothing wrong with guarding your personal space. But remember that rejecting your husband's children and being cruel is not a part of being a good wife. Motivate yourself to be a kinder and more compassionate person to your stepchildren. It doesn't mean that you have to disregard your own comfort. After a while you'll build up your own immunity to the BM Cooties, and realize you had the cure all along.

8

they're his children, but it's still your home

❖**SUCKER STEPMOM OR WICKED WITCH?**

At one time or another, most wives have fallen into either the Sucker Stepmom or the Wicked Witch category. Your ultimate goal is to recognize which one most describes your personality. After you do then you should try your best to eliminate the negative aspects so that you'll be a kinder person toward your stepchildren. By acknowledging your faults you'll avoid conflict with your husband, his children and BM. Let's explore more about these two categories.

Sucker Stepmom

Meet Sucker Stepmom. She wants her husband's children to like her. She cooks delicious meals for them, entices them with undeserved privileges and does nothing to correct their inappropriate behavior. Sucker Stepmom won't allow her husband to be the more responsible and involved adult when the children visit. Maybe her husband would like to bond more with his children, but Sucker Stepmom is always in the way. Sucker Stepmom secretly hopes that she can convince her stepchildren that she is better than BM.

BM and the stepchildren already have a lack of respect for Sucker Stepmom because she just doesn't make anyone earn her respect. Sucker Stepmom doesn't care about her right to be protected or thanked. If BM invades her space, the Sucker Stepmom just smiles. If BM sends the children to visit looking unkempt and filthy, Sucker Stepmom races to fix them up. She never complains or marks her territory. She gives herself away, accepts any kind of abuse and continuously forces herself on her husband's children. Sound like you?

Wicked Witch

The Wicked Witch is just the opposite. She didn't give birth to those critters and if they know what's good, they'd better stay out of her way. The Wicked Witch abhors her stepchildren. She doesn't care about their feelings and she certainly couldn't care less about their relationship with her husband. She married her husband, not some snot-nosed, ashy kid. The Wicked Witch openly insults BM in front of the children and does everything she can to make the children feel uncomfortable when they visit to see her husband.

The Wicked Witch lets her husband do everything with the children and is not involved in their activities. The Wicked Witch thinks the stepchildren are ugly, smelly, dirty and stupid and hates to be seen in public with them. If her husband were to forget about his children with BM, The Wicked Witch would be ecstatic. She sees the children as parasitic little fleas infringing on her life and marriage. As for BM, The Wicked Witch has no intention of ever respecting or understanding BM's problems or accomplishments. The Wicked Witch only cares about her own life. Anyone who dares alter it better come prepared for a fight.

What kind of stepmother are you? I know that the way you treat your stepchildren will have a lot to do with the way that they treat you. It's hard to be cool, calm and collected when somebody else's child thinks they can start a fire in your kitchen. There are ways to deal with disrespectful stepchildren. But what if you're just plain old prejudiced against the stepchild because of how you feel toward BM? Or what if you're so insecure about where you fit in the family that you let everyone party hardy? For your own sake there must be a balance.

QUIZ

Take this quiz to determine what kind of stepmother you are. Don't think about selecting the "right" answer. Just pick the answer that describes the action you'd most likely follow if faced with the hypothetical scenario. Be honest. You don't have to show anybody your answers if you're ashamed of them. Remember you are not being judged here, you're only finding out more about yourself.

1. Your husband steps out of the house to get some toilet paper. He leaves your 6-year-old stepdaughter with you. The minute he leaves she begins throwing a horrifying tantrum. You:

    a. observe her calmly and then tell her that her behavior is unacceptable. You tell her that the longer she cries and throws a fit, the longer she'll be in time out when your husband returns.

    b. totally ignore her, turn on your favorite CD at a high volume and surf the Internet.

    c. rush and bring her all of the toys you and your husband have bought her, as you try coaxing her to stop crying.

2. For some reason your stepchildren never finish their vegetables at your dinner table. You:

    a. smile and order a pizza almost every time, while apologetically clearing the table.

    b. tell the children that the reason they have dull skin tone and brittle fingernails is because their mother feeds them junk.

    c. explain that in your house you and your husband eat healthy foods so that you can avoid various ailments. You ask if they'd like to suggest any new ideas for healthy dinners.

3. BM only exposes your husband's children to a certain kind of music. Many times you find that this music contains suggestive or obscene lyrics. You:

   a. tell the stepchildren that only low-life savages sing those songs and if they want to watch any television they better can the trashy music.

   b. make it clear that the children aren't allowed to sing or listen to that music in your house, but you try to introduce them to other genres of music.

   c. take the children to Walmart and let them pick 2 CDs from their favorite artists. Next weekend you'll buy them CD walkmans.

4. Your husband wants to take your stepson out for dinner except that he'd like it to be just the two of them. You:

   a. and your husband get into yet another heated argument. If anything you should be the one he's taking out to dinner. God knows you deserve a trophy for dealing with his weird son.

   b. become hurt and puzzled. You do everything you can to make everyone feel like they're in one big, happy family. You don't understand why you weren't invited.

   c. help your husband find a good restaurant and tell him to have a nice time. You'd appreciate some time to yourself anyway.

5. BM calls your house and asks to speak with her daughter. You:

   a. ask BM to hold while you inform your stepdaughter that her mother is on the telephone and would like to speak with her.

   b. beam with delight and tell BM how happy you are to hear from her. You ask her if there's anything special she'd like you to do for her daughter. After your stepdaughter pries you off of the phone, you sit right next to her while she talks to BM.

   c. tell BM to hold on and "forget" to tell your stepdaughter that BM has called.

6. Your stepson makes some long distance phone calls at your home. He didn't get your husband's or your permission. You:

   a. tell your stepson not to worry about the bill and buy him his own calling card for future usage.

b. tell your stepson that you're disappointed in his actions and then show your husband the telephone bill. You and your husband decide the consequences for your stepson, but you let your husband take the lead in making the final decision.

c. call BM and demand that she use her child support money to pay the balance for the bill her son incurred, otherwise you'll file a suit against her.

7. Your own biological daughter, 6, comes crying to you and tells you that her stepsister, 10, has been hitting her and calling her names. You:

a. summon your stepdaughter and immediately begin physically threatening her. You tell her to keep her "dirty little hands" off of your daughter.

b. tell your daughter that her stepsister "didn't mean it" and that she should go back and play. It's important that your stepdaughter never feels as if you're chastising her on behalf of your own daughter.

c. get your husband, stepdaughter and daughter together to discuss the issue and find out what actually happened. Also, if you're upset you know it would be better to have your husband present anyway.

8. Your stepson mentions that his own mother can ice skate like a pro. You:

a. smile and say, "That's nice."

b. immediately make plans to take ice skating lessons.

c. shrug and say you don't care.

9. Your young stepson, 7, becomes angry when you tell him he may not watch a very popular action-packed R-rated movie. He runs up to you and spits on you. You:

a. wipe off his spit and tell him that he may watch the movie but first he must spend 10 minutes in time out.

b. slap the living daylights out of him. The hell with DYFS, you don't have to tolerate any little misfit's spit!

    c.   grab him by the arm and firmly state that he will not be allowed to spit or hit anyone in your home. You inform your husband immediately and you both decide how he will be punished.

10. Your stepdaughter has been lying to your husband about her trips to the library. She actually has been visiting a boy from school. You:

    a.   talk to your stepdaughter in hopes that she'll understand the dangers of lying about where she's been or is going. You also ask her to think about what it means to be trustworthy and responsible. You inform your husband.

    b.   secretly tell her that you'll help her to keep her future rendez-vous a secret. You promise not to tell your husband, after all, you were a teenager once yourself.

    c.   tell your husband that his daughter's well on her way to becoming a slut like her mother.

Tally your score:
1) a-2, b-3, c-1; 2) a-1, b-3, c-2; 3) a-3, b-2, c-1; 4) a-3, b-1, c-2; 5) a-2, b-1, c-3; 6) a-1, b-2, c-3; 7) a-3, b-1, c-2; 8) a-2, b-1, c-3; 9) a-1, b-3, c-2; 10) a-2, b-1, c-3

You're a Sucker (10–17)
If you don't realize that your marriage comes first and that BM's children are not and never will be YOURS, you're on your way to losing what's left of your self-esteem and your marriage. Don't worry, in this chapter you'll find great ways to begin gaining more confidence in who YOU are meant to be. BM nor your stepchildren should rob you of your dignity or take your kindness for granted. You have to overcome your fear of conflict so that your role as wife and woman of your house will be taken seriously.

If you want children then have or adopt your own! You can even volunteer at an after school or children's program if you feel the need to nurture children. By hoping to win over your stepchildren, you'll only get your feelings hurt. You are seriously overdoing it, sister.

Balanced Babe (18–24)
You do everything you can to remain fair to your husband and fair to his children. Not that you haven't stepped into the Sucker Stepmom's shoes a few times, but you've learned that you have the right to be comfortable and treated fairly. And of course BM's ignorance, your stepchildren's

defiance or maybe even your own selfishness has led you to play the Wicked Witch, too. You think all of your decisions through and make sure that you are not the family doormat. Why should you be? No one has to tell you that you're a great, compassionate woman with a right to happiness. You know already! In all of your experiences though, you've learned to put your marriage first while being aware of your own behavior. Good for you.

Put Down That Broom! (25–30)

You may think you're hurting BM and your stepchildren by being unfair and inconsiderate but in the end, you'll be the one with an ulcer and high blood pressure. You're not giving yourself a chance to enjoy your marriage. Did you walk down the aisle in a wedding dress or in camouflage clothing? You're creating an unnecessary war for yourself and your husband. If your husband married you of his free will then your stepchildren or BM can do nothing to take him away from you. Everyone needs to feel secure, but drowning yourself and those around you in vicious and mean-spirited comments and intentions is useless. Learn how to embrace being a fair wife to your husband, but first learn how to be fair with yourself. At this point you're giving yourself the short end of the stick. Now that you know which category you fall into, continue reading to find helpful tips on dealing with general occurrences during your stepchildren's visitation.

❖THE CHILDREN AND YOUR RULES

If it isn't alright with you then it shouldn't be honored or tolerated in your home. Period.

Your husband must understand that the activities or behaviors that are okay in BM's home don't have to be accepted in yours. There are certain pet peeves that you may have. Maybe you don't like the children to walk inside the home while wearing shoes. Maybe you feel strongly against your 13-year-old stepdaughter calling boys on your telephone, even though BM allows it at her house. Maybe you don't want your stepchildren singing at the dinner table. Whatever your dislikes are, it is reasonable to discuss creating rules in your home.

It's true that you aren't their mother, but as a responsible adult you must set your own standards when the children visit. You don't have to feel awkward about maintaining your home environment because even though the stepchildren are your husband's biological children—they are still in **your** home. If the average guests must learn how to be polite, gracious and respectful in their host's home, why shouldn't your stepchildren? You are part of the reason they are able to enjoy visiting with their father. Maybe you cook them wonderful meals or help pay the mortgage or light bill. Whatever your contributions are to the household, it earns you the right to ask for order from anyone who steps over your threshold.

Now before you run to chisel your rules into a stone tablet, ask yourself some questions. How do you think toddlers, preteens or teenagers should behave? Depending on the age of the child, he or she may need different boundaries and freedoms. What kind of privileges should an 8-year-old have? Should he or she have the same freedoms as a 16-year-old? Discuss your child-rearing philosophies and ideals with your husband. Try to learn as much as you can about each of your stepchildren on an individual basis. This way your rules will be easier to enforce and easier for the stepchildren to follow.

After you have a general idea of what behavior to expect from children in different age brackets, you're ready to begin making your rules. Make sure that you and your husband make these rules together. If the thought of making a detailed list of rules or a reward system overwhelms you, try making a list of general rules. Behaviors that show respect, responsibility, kindness and honesty are great pillars on which to create simple but effective rules.

As you get to know your stepchildren, and as they become more familiar with your personality, you may feel more comfortable making rules along the way. Always make sure that you give your husband a chance to understand why you'd like certain rules enforced. Your husband, as well, should freely explain why he curtails or allows certain behaviors in your home. The key in creating effective rules is presenting a united front with your husband, but you first must agree on what the rules are.

At the end of this chapter you will find a general list of rules for toddlers, young children, pre-teens and teenagers. Hopefully, you will find the rules helpful or inspirational.

Things to remember:

- You and your husband should decide what rules all children in your home will follow.

- Take into consideration the child's age and level of social and mental development when creating rules. For example, don't try to force a 4-year-old to wash her dirty dinner plate and cup after eating. The rule can be that the 4-year-old uses her napkin to wipe her face and hands while eating—you or hubby should take care of the dishes. Another example: It may be fine for a 17-year-old to have a curfew of 11:30 p.m. on weekends, but a 13-year-old should have an earlier curfew.

- A reward/consequences system is a great way to keep your rules organized and show the children that they are responsible for their actions. For example a reward for a 15-year-old doing homework without being nagged may be the privilege of speaking on the telephone for an extra half-hour past curfew. Or a consequence for a 6-year-old's rude behavior may mean no dessert or writing a small essay.

- A list of general rules for all-aged stepchildren is effective, too. Do ensure that consequences and rewards are given for the children's behavior.

- Don't become a drill sergeant. Remember that the children will need time to adjust to your expectations. Be patient and allow them to make a couple of mistakes before giving them a final warning.

- The punishments in your household should not be demeaning or cruel to your stepchildren. If Johnny, 10, gets a failing test grade do not suggest that he should wear a clown suit to the grocery store. Or if Kayla, 13, calls you a "stupid ho" under her breath do not take her to New York City's 42nd Street after midnight so that she can really understand what a "ho" is. Johnny should be made to study more, and Kayla should lose certain privileges as well as get the lecture of her life from you *and* your husband.

- Don't be too lavish with awarding good behavior. Children and adults are responsible for being respectful and considerate. For instance, if Tina cleans up her crayons after drawing and coloring, there is no need to reward her with a Toys'R'Us shopping spree. Certain behaviors should be the norm.

❖PROPER TELEPHONE ETIQUETTE

There are basically two areas that you need to make rules for concerning telephone usage. One is when your stepchildren call your house from another location, which is usually BM's home. The second area is when your stepchildren are using the telephone at your house. We'll start with the first area.

When They Call

If tensions are high between you and BM, then it is best not to hold a lengthy conversation with your stepchildren. If they call most likely they are calling to speak with your husband and should be given the opportunity to do so immediately if he is available and you are not on an important phone call.

You and your husband should decide what your standards are for phone etiquette. In some homes it's okay for a stepchild to call and say, "Is my father there?" without giving their names or a salutation. In some households any person calling should state his or her name and then ask to speak with the desired person. I believe that if a child is old enough and sophisticated enough then he or she should follow the widely accepted form of a telephone greeting, which is generally this:

> YOU: Hello?
> CHILD: Hi, this is Tamara. May I speak to my father?
> YOU: Okay Tamara, hold on a second. I'll go and get your dad.

Don't answer the phone in hopes that your stepchild will greet you with well wishes and a hearty, "Good morning, Mrs. Johnson." If they do, then kudos to their BM, at least she's taught them some kind of good manners.

If a child is too young to understand how to politely ask for his or her father, then frankly they shouldn't be using the telephone in the first place. However, some BMs do not supervise their children or take pride in the way their children behave—especially toward you, the wife. But you can work around this quirk.

> YOU: Hello?
> CHILD (five-year-old): Hi.
> YOU: Who's calling?

CHILD: Bobby.
YOU: Hi Bobby. Hold on, I'll get your father.

Notice that the wife in this scenario did not press the young child to follow the general telephone introduction that most people use. If the wife would have tried to teach the child how he should have answered the phone it might have ended up in a frustrating and useless five minutes for both stepchild and wife. Unless BM is reinforcing proper telephone etiquette in her home, it is a waste of time for you to teach her young child the rules. Remember you are not a Sucker Stepmom. Your objective is to let the child speak with your husband, do so as quickly as you can.

When your stepchild is comfortable enough with you that he or she enjoys speaking with you on the phone then indulge in a cordial conversation once in a while. Please do be aware that if BM doesn't like you, your conversation may be abruptly cut short or your stepchild may end up acting cold or strange the moment BM walks into the room. Try to refrain from becoming too attached, especially if you know that BM would not want her child speaking to you. Some stepchildren have gotten in trouble for associating with the enemy, which in this case is you.

If a stepchild, no matter the age, refuses to ask for your husband in a respectful manner then explain this to your husband and either he or both of you can speak with the child together. Inform the stepchild that he or she is welcome to call your home, but only if they do so properly. If the child is over the age of 6, then he or she should know how to make and conduct an acceptable phone call.

No one likes telephone harassment. If your stepchildren leave harassing messages or threats on your answering machine do not tolerate it at all. Immediately document the content of the message and write a memo that includes the date and time of the message. Save the message and allow your husband to hear it. Your husband should speak with the children and make sure that they understand why what they did was not acceptable.

If you are very angry and your husband hasn't spoken to the stepchild yet, don't call BM's home on a rampage. And if the stepchild calls back before you've gotten a chance to speak with your husband it is okay to tell the child that you will not tolerate abusive messages or threats. Do not make it a detailed conversation. State the facts, state your position and give your husband the telephone. Here's an example:

YOU: Hello?
CHILD: Is my dad there?

YOU: Who's calling?

CHILD: Trevor.

YOU: Trevor, yesterday you called and left a rude and nasty message on my answering machine.

CHILD: So?

YOU: So understand that although your father lives here, this is my house also. We will not tolerate foul language, abusive messages or harassing telephone conversations from you or anyone else. If you enjoy speaking with your father on this telephone, you'll need to respect my home. This is not up for discussion and I hope you understand what I'm telling you. If it happens again, there will be consequences. I'll go and get your father, hold on.

The wife in this case states the facts, her position and is not even interested in a give-and-take conversation with the stepchild. The wife also doesn't beg for an apology. Don't waste your time verbally confronting your stepchildren via the telephone. State your case in a calm but firm voice and let them speak with their father immediately. Even if your stepchildren don't believe it, anyone who calls your home and gets to hear your voice or converse with you is privileged! Don't give anyone the privilege of speaking with you or utilizing your telephone line if they don't deserve it, and that includes your stepchildren.

Sometimes a stepchild will have to face more serious consequences for being rude or nasty on the phone. You and your husband may decide to prohibit the stepchild from calling your home for a week or a month. In the meantime, your husband should continue to call them—it's just that the privilege of calling your home is taken away from the child. Why should you have an anxiety attack every time the telephone rings? You may need time to heal from something hurtful that the stepchild may have said to you. It is certainly your right to reclaim your space by taking such an action. When you feel comfortable again, you and your husband can decide how everyone should move forward.

If things go from bad to worse, you and your husband may need to find alternate methods of communication from the children. E-mail, snail mail or Instant Messaging may be a solution. In a worst-case scenario, where BM is encouraging the children to make prank phone calls or terrorize you, then your husband may have to change your telephone number and get a separate line for them to call him.

When the Stepchildren Make Calls from Your House

Can I call my mother?

A child of any age may ask you this question while they are visiting your home. To some wives this question makes them break out into a sweat. To other wives, the stepchild conversing with BM is not a problem. Neither is right or wrong because you have a right to have your own perceptions about an irate and difficult BM. But you don't have the right to severe a child's ties with his or her mother, even if it's only for a weekend.

Do allow the children to speak with BM if they ask you. If you are not comfortable giving them this permission then tell them to ask your husband. It is normal for a child of any age to want to touch base with his or her mother, so don't work yourself up into a frenzy.

It is *not* normal for a child to ask to call BM every other hour. If your stepchildren live with you then it is up to you and your husband to decide how often they should be allowed to call BM. Remember, this is not the insightful, balanced and considerate BM that you read about in magazines. This is an individual who has and will continue to disrespect your marriage, husband and you. You do not want her energy unnecessarily in your home and the fairest way to deal with this dilemma is to make a schedule. Older and more responsible children should be given more freedom to call BM, while younger children should be supervised in dialing the number and in the amount of time they spend on the telephone.

When the Stepchildren Want to Call Their Friends on Your Phone

The older your stepchildren are, the more likely they are to speak on the phone to their peers. Allowing them to speak with friends and classmates on the phone will really make their adjustment to spending time with you and your husband a lot easier.

Any child over the age of 10 should be allowed to call friends or receive phone calls from friends while visiting you and your husband. Make sure that they understand the rules that you and hubby have for this perk. There should be a time limit for phone conversation. The child should know how to properly write down a message and how to use call waiting. The child should also ask your permission before calling long distance.

You may also need to iron out even more details regarding telephone usage. At what age and for what reasons will your stepchildren be allowed to call members of the opposite sex? What time will be too late for your stepchild to receive or make phone calls? How should your stepchildren's friends introduce themselves when they call your home? Make sure that you and your husband discuss these decisions with your stepchild to avoid any misunderstandings.

As for younger children ages 4 through 9, there really isn't a need for them to spend much time on the telephone. Maybe there is a special friend that your stepchild is fond of though. It's okay to allow them to exchange a quick conversation under your or your husband's supervision. But in the case of a young child, keep in mind that you must explain proper telephone etiquette before you give the child this freedom. No adult wants to answer the telephone only to hear some incomprehensible child's voice on the other line. Your stepchild should know how to speak clearly if you are going to let him or her make phone calls. Also, explain what prank phone calls and phone games are to your young stepchildren. This way they will not attempt to entertain themselves by calling 911 and singing "Old MacDonald" to a dispatcher.

If you have a responsible stepchild between the ages of 6 and 10 then it is only fair that they get phone privileges that equal their abilities. Some young children know how to use Instant Messenger or e-mail. Talk to your husband if you think your younger stepchild should have more freedom on the telephone or with computer related communication.

When your stepchildren are with you and your husband they should have more to do than talk on the telephone. No matter what age, your stepchildren should always have something interesting to do or to learn about while they are at your home. Provide older children with computer games, puzzles, books, or offer to take them to a dance class or the park to meet friends for playing sports. Older children are still dazzled by the theater and by eating out in a restaurant. Don't just have them sitting around your home with nothing to do or look forward to.

Younger children especially deserve attention. Just because BM thinks it's okay to let the television and telephone be a companion for her children doesn't mean that you and your husband should follow suit. Have toys, planned picnics and educational television videos for the younger children. Allow them to help you make breakfast or dinner. You or your husband can give them bubble baths or have a reading day at the library. Check around for free children's exhibits at museums in your area.

Telephone use in your home is a privilege. As long as your stepchildren understand this and respect the rules that your husband and you have created, you should allow them some fun. The telephone should still be a minimal part of their visiting time with your husband.

- If BM has no respect for you, your husband or your home, then don't hold a lengthy conversation with your stepchild when he or she calls. It may be awkward for the child should BM walk in the same room or pick up the phone only to hear her son or daughter speaking to you.

- Your younger stepchildren who call your home may not know proper telephone etiquette. Don't get caught up in this, just give the phone to your husband. If the child lives with BM, then it is her responsibility to teach the child how to use the phone properly.

- Older children should know proper phone etiquette. Have your husband explain it to them so that they will use it when they call to speak with him or to leave a message.

- Rude messages, pranks or comments from your stepchildren via the telephone are absolutely unacceptable.

- You and your husband should decide the consequences for the stepchildren's rudeness or misuse of your telephone.

- Your stepchildren should be able to call BM. Depending on the age of the child, you and your husband should set the limitations.

- Your stepchildren, when they are old enough and responsible enough, should be allowed to call their friends on the telephone. They should also be able to receive phone calls.

- Using a timer is great to avoid teenagers tying up the phone line.

- If you have call waiting, your stepchildren who you've given permission to use the phone should know how activate the service and write down messages.

- Don't forget to let the stepchildren understand the details of their phone use privilege. Don't be too vague.

❖AT THE DINNER TABLE

Maybe you were taught that eating with your mouth open in front of others was utterly disgusting. What do you do when your stepson believes that the symphony and sight of his food being chewed is a grand addition to dinnertime at your house? What if you're used to the whole family sitting down to eat dinner together, but your teenaged stepdaughter thinks her dinner would be better digested in front of the television?

Dinner and other meal times in your home are a great opportunity to learn a lot about your stepchildren. But it's also a perfect opportunity to hear them complain about your cooking, see them smacking with their mouths wide open or to be completely ignored by them. It isn't always an apple pie affair at a stepmother's dinner table, but don't despair.

Even nuclear families have their challenges at the family table. Throw out your visions of the perfect family dinner scored by your favorite jazz CD, as you watch your stepchild quietly eat your delicious baked fish. Forget about your wishes to hear your stepson tell you how great your homemade bean pie is. Don't expect your stepchildren to become lovingly loquacious. They won't immediately open up about their school activities or the latest scandal in hip hop music. And please don't expect your husband's undivided attention.

Now that you've gotten rid of your romantic notions of dinner with the stepchildren, you're ready for what really might go down.

Put on a thick skin because you'll probably experience at least one incidence where your stepchild will not like what you've prepared for dinner. Get ready to be appalled at bad manners, open-mouth chewing, possibly body odor, dirty hands and more. Put your jealousy in the back seat when your husband seems to be more interested in his daughter than how hard you worked to finally get this recipe right. In time you will be recognized as the culinary and domestic goddess you are, but you'll need to have some patience. The following areas will help you cope with some challenges you might face.

Manners

Everyone is raised differently. The way you will teach your own biological children to eat at the table will be different than what a million other mothers across the world will ask of their children. By understanding this you'll understand why your stepchildren's mannerisms are different from what you'd expect. Your goal is to establish *what is* acceptable at your table.

You don't want your stepchildren to feel as if they are eating in a boot camp cafeteria. So when and how do you introduce your rules? Well, if the children are under the age of 10 you should teach them at the table. Younger children will adapt to rules if they are allowed to experience learning through action. If your 7-year-old stepdaughter gets up from the table without excusing herself, then you or your husband should stop her and tell her that she must first ask to be excused before leaving the table. Have her then ask to be excused. She will most likely remember this rule the next time she is ready to leave the table.

For older children up into their teens, you have two choices. When they begin to visit you and your husband, you can use dinnertime or breakfast as a great way to introduce the main dos and don'ts at the family table. Tell the stepchildren that you understand things may be different at BM's house and let them know that until they get used to the notion, following two sets of rules may be annoying. This way they will know that you are not expecting perfection from them right away.

How Will You Begin Your Meals?

Is there a tradition that you follow when beginning your meals? Maybe in your house it's normal to dig in and pass the peas. Or maybe your husband says a special prayer before anyone touches or tastes a morsel. Let your stepchildren know what goes down at the beginning of each meal.

Consider letting younger children assist with setting the table or calling other family members to the table. As for older children (including boys!) feel free to invite them into your kitchen to sample or critique your meal as you prepare it. Creating a warm atmosphere at family meals is very much like cooking a meal. You have to have the right recipe for a successful dish. In stepfamilies you have to prepare the dining atmosphere by easing tension and making all family members comfortable sharing such an intimate space with each other. Think about ways to warm up all family members before they get to the dining table.

The table should be clean when it's time for everyone to sit down and enjoy what you or your husband cooked. There shouldn't be any clothing hanging over chairs, loose sneakers under the table or cell phones next to plates. The lighting should allow everyone to see their eating utensils, cups and plates clearly. If you choose to have background music playing, it should not have suggestive or obscene lyrics. Music should also be at a level as not to force family members to speak loudly. If you do not encourage singing at your table, then maybe you may want to choose instrumental music. If possible all family members should have access to napkins or paper towels. These are just some suggestions that will help everyone feel comfortable at the dining room table.

What Happens While We're Eating?

That depends on what you and your husband think should happen. If you think it's okay to speak with food in your mouth as long as it's not flying into anyone's face then stick to your plan. If you believe that talking with food in your mouth leads to indigestion and the possibility of choking, then honor this rule.

Think about how family members should be seated. Will you allow anyone to slouch or rest their heads on the table? Do you prefer feet to be placed upon the floor, regardless of how much your 17-year-old stepson favors Yoga-inspired seating positions? What about using boosters for younger children who can't reach the table? Will you tell them to kneel down in their chairs or will you supply pillows, the Yellow Pages or an actual booster for their comfort?

Now that everyone is seated, take a look around. Is your 13-year-old daughter still dressed in her dirty lacrosse outfit? Does your 5-year-old stepson think that arriving shirtless to dinner makes him as popular as the latest wrestling celebrity? Does your husband think it's okay to conduct business phone calls via cellular phone while everyone else is forced to listen? Is your 16-year-old stepdaughter combing her hair or applying lip gloss at the table? How do you feel about what you see at your table?

You must decide with your husband what kinds of behavior and appearances are acceptable at your table. And both of you must set an example for the rules you expect the children to follow. So now that you've gotten everyone wearing decent clothing and sitting properly sans cell phone, here's the tricky part: What do we talk about and how do we talk to each other?

Conversing at the Table

Unless you're a part of the Osbourne rock-and-roll family, cursing is probably not allowed at your dinner table. Throwing food is also outlawed in many homes. Think about the conversation no-nos for your home and then observe what your stepchildren have to say at dinnertime. And don't be surprised if you hear mostly silence until they are more comfortable.

Encourage healthy conversation at the family table. This means that you need to make an effort to include your stepchildren. Don't passionately discuss the history of female genital mutilation if your 10-year-old stepdaughter is not mature enough to understand or comprehend the subject. Don't take up the entire dinnertime with property tax talk, when you could be asking your 15-year-old stepson about his baseball practice.

By all means don't limit your intellect or conversation topics to the point where you feel stifled at your own table. But if you're going to bring up the town meeting's highlights to your husband, take time to let your 4-year-old discuss the latest Sesame Street character. Remain balanced but don't cover up who you are and end up buried in endless conversation about Teletubbies or Pokémon.

What if you have tried to encourage healthy conversation at the table but you're met with resistance? Your stepchildren's resistance to your conversation is not necessarily rude. If you ask a question, and your stepchild appears shy or answers in one or two words, he or she may need some time to adjust to this new atmosphere.

If you ask a question and your stepchild completely ignores you, then that is rude. You and your husband should explain that it's okay to be shy or not in the mood to speak, but to completely ignore any adult (especially if you have cooked the meal!) is unacceptable. The child, no matter the age should be asked to finish his or her meal and then excused from the table.

When You Feel Like an Outsider

Your husband is laughing about your stepson's joke regarding a science class. Your stepdaughter is telling your husband how excited she is to begin college next year. And you—well you feel like a jealous outsider.

If seeing your husband tell your stepdaughter how pretty she is makes you uncomfortable, please don't clam up and excuse yourself from the table. It is going to take some time for you to adjust to accepting the relationship and bonding between your husband and his children that he had before you met him. Remember to give yourself space to acknowledge your feelings. Admit to yourself that you get jealous or feel awkward watching your husband be at ease with people (it doesn't matter that they're children) who don't seem to be at ease with you. After you've done this, try reading Chapter 7 again so that you can be reminded of the bond that he should have with his children.

You may think it's unfair, but you will have to work toward making yourself comfortable at the family table with your stepchildren. When it's just you and your husband and the biological children that you both share together the tone will be different. When your stepchildren are at the table, they will bring new dynamics and energy to the family setting. This doesn't have to be a negative experience for you once you overcome your fears of being an outsider in your own home.

Getting to know your children doesn't begin at the dinner table. If you hardly take time to show them that you are interested in their lives then naturally they will not gravitate toward you at the table. They will cling to the only other adult that they know is trustworthy and on their side—their father. Don't take it personally, they just need more time to warm up to you. And you may need more time and practice in showing them that you are interested in them as individuals. Don't be afraid to let your stepchildren get to know more about you, either. This will make them more comfortable with conversing with you anywhere and not just at the dinner table.

When Things Get Ugly at the Table

The last time you tried to interject in a conversation between your husband and your 15-year-old stepdaughter, she tritely explained that she was talking to her father—and not you. So what did you do? Did you slam your hand on the table and yell to the 15-year-old, "Well if you don't know how to have a conversation with ALL of us at this table you can take your choosy little ass and get the hell out of my house! And your father can go with you, too!"

Or maybe your youngest stepson believed that passing gas without excusing himself from the table was hilarious. So what did you do? Did you turn to your stepson, and while making the biggest grimace you could, ask, "Is this what your mother teaches you to do at the table? You're disgusting and filthy. Take your plate and eat in the kitchen, on the floor if you want to fart like a damn country dog at my dinner table!"

Could it be that the last straw for you was when you cooked that fancy dinner only to hear your 9-year-old stepdaughter tell your husband (right in front of you) that your macaroni and cheese tasted like rubber and that BM is the only person who can cook macaroni. Did your eyes turn into black stone as you threw your macaroni and cheese meal across the dining room? Did you yank the fork and cup out of your stepdaughter's hands and tell your husband to take his "ungrateful, gluttonous child back to her ghetto mother's house?"

Whatever has happened at your table, you've pretty much reached your boiling point. The cover is about to blow right off the pot and somebody's about to get burned!

But I do hope that your reactions to similar ordeals you may have faced were not as bombastic as the three above scenarios. That doesn't mean that you didn't feel like doing or saying those things. Whatever took place at your dinner table you were probably justified in feeling offended and disgusted. But you must think carefully before you respond out of anger toward your husband's children. Remember, you didn't raise them to be the apple of your eye. BM raised them with the manners that they have. Maybe you can help them grow into better dining companions and maybe even kinder family members.

Aside from having compassion for what may be an awkward time for your stepchildren you don't have to tolerate rudeness at the table. When you encounter:

Grotesque and foul behavior such as food spitting, intentional burping or passing gas or making continuous noises with food you or your husband should stop the child immediately and remove the plate of food and cup from the child's placemat. Firmly tell the child that this kind of inconsiderate and foul behavior will not be tolerated at the table. Tell the child to clean up whatever mess he or she has made and then give the child a choice. The child can either stay at the table and continue to eat in a civilized manner or go to his/her room, wait until everyone else has finished eating—and then return to the table to finish dinner ALONE. Let the child know the future consequences for repeating this kind of behavior.

Blatantly rude remarks intended to alienate you such as, "I wasn't talking to you" or "Why do you always have to butt in?" or rude behavior such as rolling eyes, sucking teeth, sarcastic grunting or scoffing you or your husband should stop all eating activity at the table immediately. Ask the child why she thinks it is necessary to be rude to you. When the child answers, your husband can and should respond. YOU, however, must absolutely tell the child that you understand what having a bad day means/not living with both parents may be difficult/etc. but you will not accept being spoken to in a disrespectful tone. Tell the child that everyone at the table has a right to feel comfortable and included, and that since it is your house and you try to make her feel at ease, she is expected to repay that favor with respect. If the child refuses to comply with you and your husband's requests, please excuse her from the table and have her finish her meal after everyone else is finished.

Unfair and intentionally hurtful comparisons to BM's cooking or comments such as "I hate this food," "I wanna go home," or "This dinner time is full of crap" you or your husband should stop all eating activity at the table immediately. Let the child know it's okay if he or she enjoys and loves BM's cooking. But while they are guests in your home they will eat at the table and refrain from making those kinds of hurtful remarks. Tell them that you tried to make sure that the meal was nutritious and pleasant for them. Mention that you are willing to try making new meals based on their suggestions, BUT first they must lose the nasty attitude. Ask them if they would like to be excused from the table or if they would like to continue eating in a civilized and respectful fashion.

Some of the consequences for your stepchildren's rude behavior may seem harsh, but the more you tolerate nasty behavior the more *your* blood pressure will rise and the less harmonious things will be in your house.

It is very important to acknowledge when your stepchild's behavior improves. You or your husband, or both of you together, can privately thank

the child for trying harder during this time of adjustment. Assure the child that he or she is not the only person learning how to deal with the new dynamics of the family and that if he or she ever needs to talk, that both of you are available.

Here are some tips to remember at the dinner table. In general:

- Dinnertime and other meal times in your home are a great opportunity to learn a lot about your stepchildren.

- If family time at the table doesn't start out as perfect as you imagined it's okay.

- The manners that you were taught to have at the table will be different from the manners that BM may have instilled in your stepchildren.

- Identify the behavior that is acceptable from your stepchildren. Then identify what you would like to see them change. You and your husband will decide how to explain your expectations to the stepchildren.

- Try to warm up the family before everyone gathers at the table. A cold and distant atmosphere won't be pleasant.

- Administer consequences for rude behavior and praise behavior when it improves.

- Having a special tradition at the beginning of each meal, or even at the end will make family time at the table more relaxed and positive.

- If a comment from your stepchild really incenses you, don't ever lose your cool at the family table. Don't yell, don't throw anything and don't tell the child to get out of your dining room. Refer to the methods of suggested discipline for the scenario that best fits what you have been experiencing.

- Do have a clean area for the family to eat in. Physical comfort will add to creating a comfortable atmosphere.

- You are not BM. Don't try to cook like her or create family table traditions like hers. You deserve your own unique space. It's okay to cook lasagna because your stepchildren like it when BM cooks it, but under no circumstances should you expect your food to taste like hers. Your stepchildren won't think you are more of a mother because you've done so. You are yourself and if you refuse to cook chitterlings or hot dogs for dinner—then your stepchild must and will get used to what goes down in YOUR kitchen and dining room.

- Hey, let your husband give his children some attention. Learn more about the children so that you can begin to join certain conversations instead of feeling like an outsider.

For Young Stepchildren:

- Don't bombard them with rules. Instead while they are eating correct their behavior when it happens. Teach/tell them what to do instead.

- Explain to them that following two different sets of rules may be difficult, but you'll help them to adjust.

- Younger children may enjoy small tasks such as passing out forks and cups. Maybe they can write down "tonight's menu" on a special blackboard. Make them feel involved, but do not give them any tasks that are too difficult or dangerous. No 6-year-old should be donning potholder mittens as she brings in the pot of curried chicken from the kitchen.

For Older Stepchildren:

- Give them space to show you and your husband that they can be well behaved and pleasant at the table.

- If you like, before your first meal or after you've observed them at a few meals, you and hubby can give them an informal overview of what happens at the table i.e., no gum-chewing, yoga poses or foul language.

- This is a great opportunity to have your older stepchildren participate in preparing the dinner (don't force them) or in leading the family traditions of the table.

- Have a special night to let your 16-year-old stepson or daughter prepare a meal, or suggest a new restaurant.

❖TELEVISION AND MUSIC: DECIDING WHAT'S APPROPRIATE

BM lets her 5-year-old daughter watch Jay-Z videos and sing along to suggestive lyrics that demean women. Talk shows, soap operas and even rated-R films are your stepdaughter's companion while BM talks on the phone or has company. So when you try to introduce your stepdaughter to the world of Bill Cosby's "Little Bill," you notice she is easily distracted.

Your stepson is in high school. At BM's house he is allowed to watch movies with an overabundance of foul language and graphic sexual situations. He doesn't use a Walkman to listen to his rock music. In fact, BM bought him his own stereo set so that he can blast Marilyn Manson to the fullest. When your husband asked him not to play Mr. Manson in *your* home, your stepson retaliated by throwing a tantrum and demanding to go back to BM's house.

It's your house and I know it seems as if your opinion on what's suitable for your stepchildren will always meet resistance. BM has raised the children to enjoy certain kinds of entertainment. So how will "Little Bill" survive as you attempt to ban soft-porn music videos in your house?

BM's negligence of her children's mental and social development is **abuse**. Children shouldn't be deprived of their innocence by being exposed to information or behavior that is too complex for them to dissect. If your stepchildren have been raised by the television, the radio or the movie theater then consider this as an opportunity to expose them to what you'd like any child or teenager to learn about.

Life Doesn't Equal TV or the Radio

Under normal circumstances, there is no reason that a child of any age should spend hours watching television or listening to music. Children should be taught to expand their horizons, even if they must be gently nudged at first. Once your stepchildren learn that there is a world beyond Saturday morning cartoons and Funkmaster Flex remixes, they will probably be very excited to know that you and your husband take such great interest in them.

It's not your stepchildren's fault that they were taught to inhale the worst that pop culture has to offer. Set out to introduce them to more positive outlets for entertainment. If you do this you won't be emulating a Sucker Stepmom. You'll only be doing what any caring adult would do to enhance a child's life.

You and your husband should have an idea of what kind of activities you'd like to expose the children to. Brainstorm about local museums, bookstores, parks and other venues that you think would be great for family outings. Depending on your stepchild's age, look into classes that nearby universities or other educational centers offer on weekends or after school. You will find computer courses, dance classes and art instruction for children of all ages if you look hard enough. You can't demand that your stepchildren forget about the forms of entertainment that they like if you don't offer them an alternative. You and your husband must offer enriching and fun activities if you want to interest his children.

Who Gets to Watch What?

Clearly an afternoon at the state aquarium is more enriching for an 11-year-old than an afternoon with Ricki Lake. It's your home and you and your husband must decide what the children will be exposed to when they are with you.

Ages 18 months to 3:

There are television programs specifically geared toward the attention span of toddlers. Check with your local cable company and also with the programming schedule of your local public broadcasting station. You and your husband can rent an array of videos from your local library for free, or you can purchase them from stores that sell children's entertainment. Your chosen programs should not include foul language, frightening or violent scenes or sexual situations.

Ages 4 to 8:

For this age group a wider variety of television and movie productions are available. The content of these programs may span fun and slightly scary plots, slapstick humor or educational entertainment. Check with your local cable company and your local public broadcasting station for programming schedules and descriptions. These programs should not include foul language, frightening or violent scenes or sexual situations.

Ages 9 to 12:

In this age group children are beginning to become aware of budding hormones, violence in society and other topics that may not have been of concern to them when they were younger. The programs that you and your husband allow the children to watch should not shield them from the general ills of society, but should not prematurely thrust them into analyzing content that is too intense for them. Be weary of programs that have an abundance of sexual situations, bodily exposure, sexual and/or emotional abuse between adults, heavy violence or foul language. Children at this age and younger may attempt to emulate behavior that they see on the big screen. You and your husband should at least offer them positive characters to learn from.

Ages 13 to 16:

Teenagers are not babies and you won't be able to convince them that Sesame Street or afternoon cartoons should be their television show options. In the programming you and your husband select or approve of, try to limit the amount of foul language, sexual situations and violence that your teenage stepchildren view. If they do learn about sex it should be through a heart-to-heart talk with a parent or stepparent—not from an HBO "Real Sex" series. As long as they understand that violence and horror scenes are done with special effects then they should be able to handle a general murder scene or thrilling villain chase. But sometimes movies cut off one too many hands and slit one too many throats. Don't think that teens don't have nightmares. Give the teens room, but you and your husband should be comfortable with what you've allowed them to watch.

Ages 17 and up:

It literally isn't against the law if your 17-year-old stepchild wants to check out an R-rated movie. You or your husband should be able to discuss many of the sexually racy and overtly violent scenes in some of today's blockbuster movies with your teen. I don't mean a chummy discussion over a burger and fries. I mean a serious discussion where you talk about the consequences of one night stands, senseless killing and drug abuse. These themes are common in independent films as well as the ones that feature Academy Award winning actors and actresses. There will be a time that parents have to begin to let go and allow their children to choose movies and television programming independently.

The Music That They'll Hear

One day my husband's daughter and son, who were 6 and 9-years-old at the time, were singing a Ludacris song that included the word *hoes*. In street lingo, the word *hoes* is another word for *whores*. You can imagine my disgust when I heard them singing this song as if it were Elmo's latest hit. It wasn't my fault that at BM's home they were exposed to this kind of music, yet I was forced to witness two young children sing a song that even I, an adult, found to be annoying and offensive. How do you make sure that your stepchildren don't bring the ugliness of BM's world into yours?

The first part of this answer is that you can't stop your stepchildren from singing the songs that they are allowed to listen to when they are with BM. Which leads to the second answer: They *will* bring their own musical likes and dislikes to your home and you might not the tunes they'll be singing, so to speak. But you can't stop what BM has sanctioned in her world. This is what your stepchildren have probably learned to like ever since they were old enough to sing and dance.

So when I heard my husband's two children singing the Ludacris song I nearly fainted like the Broadway drama queen I am known to be. But after I popped my eyeballs back into their sockets I simply explained to them that a *hoe* was not a person for children to sing about and that a *hoe* was a very nasty person. I didn't even get into what Webster's definition of a *hoe* was because that was just too much information for the children to handle. I was even more disgusted when my husband's daughter told me that someone told her that the word *hoes* in this particular song was actually referring to a water hose.

In any case, my objective was to have them understand that when they are with their father and me, they wouldn't be singing this song. We then altered the song's melody so that they could insert their own lyrics about toys and books. Eventually they ended up singing a different kiddie song anyway.

Don't break your back to make sure that your stepchildren never sing or listen to music that you disapprove of. You won't be with them 24 hours a day. Even a biological parent doesn't have that kind of control over their children. You didn't raise your stepchildren and trust me, as long as they are being fed rotten garbage for musical recreation elsewhere, there's not much you can do as a non-custodial stepmother. The key is to make sure that you don't have to witness or become offended if your stepchildren indulge in musical material that you or your husband dislike.

If you really don't care what your stepchild listens to then I can't say it's a crime, but their musical influences will have an affect on their behavior. The more you and your husband promote listening to positive, unique and non-violent artists, the more your stepchildren will be open to discovering new music. You aren't trying to turn them into miniature versions of adults who appreciate Bob Marley, Tito Puente, Celine Dion or Nancy Wilson. But it won't hurt them to hear something fresh and new when they visit you and their father.

Familiarize Yourself With The Trends

How can you condemn certain music if you don't have any proof that the content is negative? If you have stepchildren then you should ask them who their favorite artists are. You'd be surprised to know what artists your husband's children may like. Perhaps you have some musical interests in common or maybe they could introduce you to a new artist that you'd enjoy.

If you and your husband discover that his 15-year-old enjoys listening to music that degrades women and praises drug dealers then you have every right to forbid this in your home. But what alternative will you offer your stepson? Most rap artists have clean or edited versions of their music, so you can always leverage with this option. Maybe if your stepchild is mature enough you can allow them to listen to whatever they want, as long as they use headphones. Don't waste your energy trying to micromanage your stepchild's choice of music if a compromise can be made.

For younger stepchildren it wouldn't hurt to provide them with a collection of children's songs or fun popular music that contains non-offensive lyrics. The younger the children are the more control you will have over what they listen to while visiting you and your husband.

Keep an eye out for the popular singers of the time. You'll see them on the magazine rack at the grocery store. Check out MTV every once in a while. You won't become an expert on heavy metal, popular or rap music of the current time, but at least you'll have an idea of who your stepchildren are listening to or trying to imitate. You may discover that an artist you thought had no talent is worth listening to after all.

In deciding what your stepchildren should be allowed to watch or listen to you and your husband should:

- Take into account their physical ages and current level of mental and social development before you expose them to various entertainment mediums.

- Don't be pressured into letting them watch programs or listen to music that is trendy if it violates the tone of your household or your morals.

- Offer realistic alternatives to some of the poor entertainment choices that your stepchildren gravitate toward. For instance, if a 14-year-old wants to listen to Lil' Kim then don't force her to listen to Carly Simon's Greatest Hits. It doesn't make any sense! Offer to buy her an edited version of the Lil' Kim CD or a different, but less crass CD all together. Make her understand why Lil' Kim is not respected in your household. The same goes for younger children. Offer them alternatives that are attractive—don't make them trade in Ashanti for a taste of zydeco music (unless they're from Louisiana and you know they'll like it).

- Know what your stepchildren enjoy. Who are their favorite movie stars and musicians? Look out for tidbits of trendy entertainers on magazine stands, on music video channels or in your newspaper's entertainment section.

- You're not their cultural savior. Please don't try to change or force your step-children to like classical or calypso music so that they can fit your expectations of what children should be like. Torture your own biological children with the must-have picks of your home. If they appear to be interested in your music then share it with them, if not don't bombard them with too much.

• Accept that they will be exposed to whatever BM thinks is okay. All you can do is hope that the children don't become socially stunted by the images and music that BM allows.

• Your stepchildren may think that you and your husband are stiff, boring and corny but that BM is cool. So what? We all are allowed to have opinions. They will have their opinions about you, and you certainly will have your feelings about them. Your job is to make sure that your stepchildren stay within bounds while at your house. Being cool shouldn't be your priority.

• You and your husband are helping your stepchildren learn that there is a world outside of BM's box and that there are so many different forms of entertainment to discover.

❖RELIGIOUS DIFFERENCES

If you and your husband practice a different religion than your stepchildren then you may run into a few conflicts. How should you all pray at the family table? What about attending a religious service? Should your stepchildren be forced to attend your mosque, church or synagogue? Whose religious freedom and comfort is more important?

My husband's son would sing Christmas carols at the table while my step-daughter would leave phone messages that said "Happy Halloween!" My husband and I don't celebrate either one of these holidays, so how did we handle it?

In blended families there always has to be a level of democracy, even with religious beliefs. Most children follow the same path of spirituality that their parents choose, but there are exceptions when the children don't live with one of their parents. The key is finding a balance so that the stepchildren are not ashamed of their religion, while making sure that your spiritual beliefs are not overshadowed.

This is a very fragile area so I can only offer general guidelines. You and your husband will have to iron out more of the wrinkles and may want to consult with a respected religious member of your community to seek more specific advice.

• Decide if you will allow your children to say their own prayer at mealtimes after you and your household members have said yours.

- Decide if you think your stepchildren should sing religious songs at your home. If these songs will offend your family or confuse your own biological children then you are under no obligation to allow it.

- If your stepchildren are greatly involved in their own religious community, then you and your husband must decide if your should thrust them into your own community. The older the children are, the more freedom you should give them in helping you to make this choice.

- Don't put any pressure on your stepchildren to convert them to your way of life.

- Don't allow the religious beliefs that BM has instilled in your stepchildren to persuade your spiritual or religion-related decisions.

- As long as you aren't offended and your own biological children are not being shortchanged, let your husband make the final decisions about your stepchildren's religious expression at your house.

❖STEPCHILDREN OR NOT: IT'S YOUR HOUSE

As promised here is a list of general rules that you can use no matter how old your stepchildren are. Copy the rules down on a poster board and decorate it before putting it in a place that everyone can see it.

1. Be kind, so that others will be kind to you.

2. "Thank you," "you're welcome," and "please" are used in this house.

3. If you make a mess, clean it up.

4. Don't be afraid to ask for help if you need it.

5. If you don't have permission, ask for it before you do something on your own.

6. Respect everyone and their personal belongings in this house (even the cat's).

7. Please share your ideas and feelings.

8. Be thankful for your blessings.

You wouldn't let a stranger come into your house and turn it topsy-turvy would you? Stepchildren are very similar to strangers in that they aren't always fully aware of the mood or tone of your home. They may not understand your lifestyle and they may not care if they disrupt it! And yes, you do become a host when your stepchildren visit. You should do your best to make them feel comfortable and welcome.

We all know that stepchildren carry a bit more clout than strangers or guests. They are our husband's children. They must accept us as more than a temporary part of their father's life. We must also accept them as part of our husband's past, present and future. But it is your home and you don't have to accept them if they behave like miniature revolutionaries or guerillas, either. Your stepchildren must respect your house in order for them to fully enjoy visiting their father.

Receiving your stepchildren into your home is a constant learning experience. It will be trying at times, and at other times fun and rewarding. You will have to repeat yourself and explain your philosophies to children who may have been raised in a manner totally oblivious to your morals. You will be thought of as mean sometimes. Your stepchildren may give you major attitude and back talk.

Give yourself and your stepchildren a window of time to adjust. If you try to lay down the law and you catch flack from your stepchildren or even indirectly from BM, don't back down. It is your home and your husband's. Without apologies, you should both decide what flies and what flunks in your house. Remember to always have one hand extended in friendship and guidance, while using the other hand to reroute what you'd rather not have in your life when your stepchildren are with you.

9

when enough is enough

❖WHEN YOUR HUSBAND HAS TO RETREAT FROM HIS EX

In an ideal world the ugly problems between exes shouldn't and don't ever affect the children involved. In the real world if BM is simply too crazy or violent with your husband or you, your husband may decide to cut her totally out of his life. Just because your husband had children with BM doesn't mean that he must endure a life of humiliating and socially paralyzing drama at her hands.

The children will most certainly feel this blow the hardest. And although you may have empathy for the children, it is not your responsibility to make their mother behave properly. A smart BM knows that she needs to be an amicable person toward her children's father and yes, his wife, so that the children will receive the best experience amid their parent's breakup.

My husband and I dealt with BM's slander and rudeness. We lived through her spiteful indoctrination of her own children so that they would hold a grudge against me. My husband was even affected by **parental alienation syndrome** as a result of BM's selfishness. Parental alienation syndrome happens when the custodial parent attempts to drive a wedge between the child and the non-custodial parent. Here is a definition:

> Parental alienation is the creation of a singular relationship between a child and one parent, while this said parent purposely excludes the other parent. The fully alienated child is a child who doesn't want to have any contact whatsoever with one parent and who expresses only negative feelings for that parent and only positive feelings for the other parent. This child has lost the range of feelings for both parents that is normal for a child.

Some examples and results of parental alienation syndrome are:

- BM tells her children that their father doesn't love them anymore.

- BM tries to convince her children's teacher or school that your husband shouldn't have access to the child's academic progress without her permission.

- The children are brainwashed into believing that their father is the "bad" parent, while BM takes on the role of the "good" parent.

- BM threatens your husband with not being able to contact or see his children.

- Your husband's children are afraid to call him whenever BM is around, so eventually they don't call anymore.

- Your husband's children will lie about your husband's treatment of them to please BM.

My husband and I have experienced all of the above because of BM's ignorance. It's so distressing that crazy people can procreate. Anyway, we tried our best to teach my husband's children right from wrong without bad-mouthing their mother or putting too much pressure on them. But when BM began threatening violence against me and my husband, we knew that we couldn't risk our safety for the sake of visitation with his children. When we were denied a restraining order, we decided to indefinitely remove BM from our life.

The BM I had to deal with even had the audacity to suggest that my husband could only see his children on the condition that I was not present. So in addition to facing her threats of violence, she actually believed that she had the power to use her children to drive a wedge between my husband and me. She was sadly mistaken because we were not having any of that.

Still BM refused to behave herself. She didn't comply with the court order that allowed my husband full weekend visitation. "F*ck the courts! I do what I want to do!" she told my husband. This is the kind of reckless behavior that many married couples have to deal with concerning a BM.

When my husband and I found out we were going to have our first baby we were not going to risk my well-being or our unborn baby's health by letting BM stress us out. She was simply not healthy enough to remain in our lives. At this point who knows if she'll ever get an invitation to come back?

Sometimes we have to let go of people. If you had a family member who stole from you would you let this person spend the night in your home? Of course not, that is, unless you have a masochistic fetish for being robbed. So why should you or your husband allow a potentially dangerous person such as BM to remain in your lives? When BM becomes a social liability you do have the right to shut the door in her face.

If you and your husband take this step here are three questions that are sure to surface from people you know. Here are some solutions and answers.

If your husband doesn't maintain contact with BM isn't he overlooking his children's need to have him in their lives?

Your husband can't be a good father if he ends up in jail, the hospital or even dead because of drama with BM. Your husband can't be a good father if his children constantly witness him and BM fighting all the time. Also, if the children witness BM threatening violence toward you or your husband they get nothing out of seeing you and your husband enduring this. There are ways that your husband can see his children without having to deal with BM.

Can't your husband excuse BM's behavior and just make it a goal to connect with his children?

No one asks women who are victims of verbal, physical or emotional abuse to excuse the behavior of abusive husbands so that their children can remain in a two-parent household. What makes anyone think that your husband must ignore his or your needs for respect, comfort and safety so that BM can feel satisfied? You husband will only be able to have the utmost peaceful and sane connection with his children when BM gets her act together. Until then there will always be the underlying presence of BM's hostility whenever your husband connects with his children.

If you and your husband decide to cut BM out of your lives, you're giving her just what she wants, aren't you?

That depends. Some BMs want their children's father out of their lives so that they can smoothly transition into a new relationship. They are so insecure that they will overlook the importance of their children's connection to their biological father in lieu of getting their groove on with anyone who will offer to dance. Some BMs fear that their new boyfriends will leave them if your husband plays an active role in his children's lives. If this is what BM wants then she'll have to face karma when it comes back to knock her upside the head. These are her issues not yours. Your goal is to have a peaceful drama-free life and whatever effect this has on BM's pleasure is not your concern.

But there are also BMs who can't fathom being exiled from your husband's life. This is because the attention, albeit negative, that you and your husband give her validates her. Your reactions to her rudeness, temper tantrums and ill behavior really turn some BMs on. So in blocking BM out of your life you'll notice that she might even try to burrow her way back in! How dare you and your husband demand an end to her erratic behavior? Don't be surprised if BM even denies her own faults and accuses *your* husband of alienating their children.

❖GREAT WAYS FOR DAD TO STAY IN TOUCH WITH HIS KIDS

If your husband has come to a dead end in the co-parenting relationship with BM, out of his frustration he may wish to cut ties with her, yet remain a part of his children's lives. But if he doesn't call BM's house or even go to BM's house to pick his children up for visitation then how will he maintain the bond with his children? Here are some ways.

Dad Should Be an Active Parent in His Children's School

Teachers really appreciate it when a parent goes above and beyond the expectations of the school. Your husband should volunteer to chaperone class trips, attend board of education meetings, read to his child's class or even donate educational games to the classroom. All of these activities will show the authorities at the school that your husband has good intentions concerning his children. In addition, at least every two to three months your husband should schedule meetings with the teachers to discuss the progress of his children. Your husband will become a respected member of the educational community while being able to see his child through school activities.

Email and Snail Mail

If your husband's children are old enough then they can always correspond through email or by writing letters. Hopefully your stepchildren will not be punished for corresponding with their father. When birthdays come around your husband can send gifts, flowers and other goodies through a mail service. You don't even have to wait for a special occasion, a card that simply says 'I Miss You' will bring a smile to the children. If you or your husband suspects that contacting the children through these methods will get them in trouble with BM then try to find a different way to connect with them.

Pickups and Drop-Offs at Neutral Locations

Some BMs are always in the mood for a ghetto brawl or argument. Your husband may have had to face this kind of behavior as he is going to drop off or pick up his children for visitation. To put an end to all of this your husband could try to petition family court to allow for third-party pickups and drop-offs. For instance, instead of picking up the children from BM's house BM might be ordered to meet your husband at the local police station with the children for the visitation pickup and drop off. By meeting BM on the neutral grounds of the police department your husband has a good chance of avoiding any unsuitable Baby's Mama Drama. A police station isn't your husband's only option. Maybe a library or a public landmark would be better if your husband thinks BM will maintain her temper. Otherwise, aim for the police station.

Third Party Visitations

What if your husband doesn't want to see BM at all? Maybe BM has a kind family member who is willing to drop off the children at your home or else meet your husband at a place where he can pick up the children. BM would have to agree to these terms, preferably in court and in writing. If she is concerned at all about the bond between her children and your husband then she will oblige. In an extreme case, your husband may want to actually visit with the children at a third party's residence if he fears that BM will use their children as an excuse to bumrush his home.

Telephone Calls

If your husband's children spend a lot of time at their grandmother's or a baby sitter's house then perhaps your husband can call them at these places to say hello. Many husbands do not want to call BM's house because of all of the negative energy they have to face. By finding a different way to reach out to the children, a more relaxed and peaceful atmosphere can be expected. The children and their father will be more comfortable speaking to each other without worrying about whether or not BM will act out or say something nasty in the background.

❖WHAT HAPPENS IN THE END?

First of all, you shouldn't have to force your husband to ban BM from your lives if she is actually a dangerous and toxic person. It's true you can demand that your husband do everything he can to ensure that your home is a safe haven for you, but ultimately this is his decision and responsibility.

If your husband decides to make this decision then don't take his strength for granted. He knows that by blocking BM from his life the tradeoff will be the ease with which he is allowed to interact with his children. At the same time he is a grown man and no adult should have to walk on eggshells for the sake of this kind of nonsense. As his wife you definitely are worthy of this sacrifice. It isn't your fault if his children don't get to interact with their father on better terms. BM must learn to shape up her behavior for the sake of her children. They are HER children and this is HER task to conquer.

Eventually BM may decide that she should tone down the circus act and pave the way for a good co-parenting relationship with her children's father. If you and your husband think that she has changed enough to allow her to call your home or approach your doorstep then consider yourself very lucky. If BM does move beyond her animosity then try to forgive her and give her some credit. Her journey to self-improvement was probably not easy. Most importantly her children will have the opportunity to love their father freely, as all children should.

10

starting a family with your husband

❖You'll Be a Wonderful Mom (if you aren't already)

Many women who are not yet parents themselves marry men who have children from previous relationships. Jada Pinkett-Smith, Catherine Zeta Jones, Amy Yasbeck (the late John Ritter's wife) and even Whitney Houston are all well-known women who had their first child with a husband who was already a parent. You aren't the only woman who's stepped into what can be a sticky and very sensitive area.

You may want more than anything to expand your family with your husband. Maybe you daydream about what a child of yours and his would look like. You fantasize about the things you will do together as a family without having to deal with the Baby's Mama Drama. But at the back of your mind, fear evokes some questions and concerns.

Will I be a good mother? I know I asked myself this question many times before I even became pregnant with my daughter. I examined how critical I was of BM and the way she raised my husband's two children. I thought about the many times my husband's daughter's hair wasn't combed or the behavior I witnessed from my husband's son. I thought about the many times I said to myself, "My son or daughter would never do that!" or "I would never do such and such to my children!" I was really the BM Critic of the Century.

Suddenly when I was pregnant and on my way to motherhood I wondered if my judgments upon BM were too harsh. I mean what if I was having a hectic week and my daughter had to wear the same frizzy cornrows to school for days? (I don't think this would ever happen, though) Would people think that I was some self-centered negligent mother? I wondered if I could live up to the same high standards of parenting that I used to assess BM's mothering skills.

Although you may be overly idealistic about what a good mother should be, if you were brought up with good standards and self-respect then you *will* be a wonderful mother. Don't feel guilty about having made judgments against BM if she was in fact shortchanging your stepchildren. This is what will make you a good mother—the ability to define what a good mother ISN'T.

So yes, you may not have any children with your husband yet, but just the fact that you are passionate about keeping Baby Mama Drama out of your marriage shows a lot about the kind of woman you are. It shows that you work hard to create a good and peaceful life for yourself and those you love. It shows that you are ready and willing to always travel the high road. What child wouldn't be lucky to have you for a mother? The strength you have exerted in having to deal with a BM while maintaining your marriage shows that you have the patience and insight to be the cornerstone of a beautiful family.

If you have a high regard for the privilege of parenthood, then you and your husband will operate around those standards. Chances are that any children born to you and your husband will know what it means to be purely loved by two parents. You and your husband will help each other evolve into wiser parents throughout the years. You'll both use what you've learned regarding BM's wacky parenting as guidelines for how you DON'T want any children under your care to be raised. So save your anxiety for the real trials of motherhood. You'll have so much more to really concern yourself with like whether or not you'll breastfeed, which pamper brand is best and so much more!

- It's normal to feel some anxiety about experiencing motherhood with your husband.

- If you have high standards for good parenting then it will be evident in the way you raise your children.

- There will be times when you may not be the perfect mother, but it doesn't mean you are a bad mother.

- BM's manner of raising her children will be different from yours, and even though you may not agree with BM's methods, concentrate on constantly improving your own.

- Trust that you and your husband will help each other raise a harmonious family.

- You will be a good mother.

❖ DON'T WORRY. HE'LL LOVE YOUR BABY, TOO

Maybe you wish that you were the first woman to have your husband's children. Well, that just wasn't written in your horoscope. Your life's path has probably allowed you to accomplish other great things besides having children. So although it will be your first time as a biological mother to your husband's children, this is like a second chance at success for your husband. Sometimes taking a second chance is the only way for someone to experience success. That's what your husband did when he married you.

We all know that having children is a physical accomplishment that many people (some deserving and some not) are capable of doing. The hard part is raising a harmonious family under the directorship of two compatible and loving parents. You and your husband are obviously compatible and loving, wonderful ingredients for the recipe of childrearing. It doesn't mean that your husband will love his children with BM any less, but raising children with you will be a different experience for him.

When a father is free to love his children without the negative energy of a violent, money-hungry, rude or drug-addicted BM the experience is so much more rewarding for all family members involved. If a BM constantly speaks ill of her children's father or his wife then the children become confused about how they should feel toward these special adults in their life. The children are not given the freedom to love their father unconditionally, and in turn the father is not given the chance to give his children all that he wishes he could.

If you and your husband decide to become parents then the barriers that BM's silly attitudes and behaviors produce will be absent. Your husband will now be able to educate, love, chastise and parent a child who won't be afraid to love him back. You will be able to love and nurture a child without worrying about how BM will react, because this will be *your* child. This will be so much more of a pleasant experience in contrast to the incidents that may sometimes arise when your stepchildren are involved. If BM wanted the same beneficial atmosphere for her children, then she would have chosen to be a positive parent instead. As a result of BM's selfishness her children get a relationship with their father that lacks quality.

You might wonder if your husband's attachment to his children with BM will make him less attached to the child you have together. Your husband should have a special bond with each of his children, including the ones he had with BM. This is not your area to dictate. But just because your husband has special memories and history with his older child or children with BM, it doesn't mean that your child will receive anything less. In fact, because you and your husband are conscious partners, your child may create even more memories and gain more experience with your husband. The simple fact that **your child will live with both parents all of the time** will have a great effect on the bond that he or she will have with your husband.

Instead of worrying about whether your husband has exhausted all of his Delightful Daddy energy, try thinking about all of the things you will do together as a family. Envision your husband feeding your baby his first cup of applesauce. Imagine the picnics in the park you'll plan together as a family. Think about how well you'll work as a team when it comes to disciplining your children. Can you see the endless possibilities?

At least your children can get a big hug from your husband in the middle of the night when they are frightened by the monsters under their beds. Your children can go grocery shopping or snow sledding with your husband without wondering if they are being disloyal to their mother. They won't worry about what time they must return to their "other" home. It really will be okay. Your husband will love your children, too. Why? Because they will witness a mother who loves and respects their father, and a father who will be able to prove that he deserves to be very loved by his children. You are going to help bring him these very special blessings, so be proud of the important role you have.

- It was not your destiny to be the first woman to bear your husband's children. But you can be the first woman to raise a harmonious family with him.

- Your husband's history and memories with his first set of children will not lower the quality of his relationship with the children you have together.

- Envision the positive things that your children will be able to do with your husband.

- Your children will live in a home with two loving parents. Be happy about that.

- Your husband will be so grateful to receive unconditional love from your children. It's something that every good father deserves.

- Your children will get to know their father on a more intimate basis and therefore create intimate memories and history.

❖Budgeting for New Baby

Once you and your husband do have a new baby, you'll probably have to make some changes in your budget, especially if you decide to become a stay-at-home mother. The first thing you and your husband should decide before your baby's even born is whether or not you'd like to pursue a downward modification in child support.

In many states this is looked at as a change in circumstance for the non-custodial parent, which your husband probably is. Most husbands are non-custodial parents in the United States. Depending on whether or not the modification would be substantial, your husband may or may not want to go back to court. A lawyer would be the best advisor on what your husband's child support bill would look like after your baby's born.

So after you and your husband decide on how you'd like to handle your child support issues, you're going to have to rework your budget, too. All of a sudden you'll have new items to buy for a baby. Things like pampers, baby clothing and bottles are necessities and will take priority over your cable television subscription. Here are some ideas on how to cut costs.

Entertainment

- Rent movies instead of paying a babysitter to watch the baby while you go out to the movie theater.

- Downgrade your premium cable channels to the basic selection.

- Buy used CDs from amazon.com or go to a used CD store.

- Burn your favorite CDs from your friends.

- Ditch the DSL or cable Internet connection for a cheaper dial-up Internet provider.

- Put a block on your phone for long distance and keep a bargain calling card handy. If you can find a cheap phone service package for unlimited and local long distance then sign up for it.

Meals

- Actually cook the food that you buy at the supermarket! Don't let it wilt away in your refrigerator.

- Plan ahead with your husband if you want to have a special night out at a restaurant and decide how much your budget will allow you to spend.

- Store your leftover dinner in Tupperware so that you or your husband can have the meal for lunch.

- Make breakfast every morning. You and your husband don't need to waste money on expensive muffins and over-priced tea and coffee at the local deli.

- Bring your favorite tea bags with you when you go out, that way all you'll need is hot water and a sweetener if you get the urge to have a cup of tea.

- Instead of buying cakes and pies, try making your own.

Clothes

- Don't be ashamed to buy your baby's, husband's or your own clothing from a thrift store. Some of the clothes have never even been worn and if they have they are in very good shape and for a lot less!

- Purchase the clothing that you will need, not clothes that you'll only wear once.

- Until you start working again full-time, all you really need are four pairs of shoes. A black pair, a brown pair, a black pair of pumps and a pair of good sneakers.

Looking Good

- Instead of getting your hair done professionally all of the time, try doing it yourself half of the time.

- Skip the spa treatments and turn your bathroom into a peaceful oasis. Stock your shelves with sweet-smelling lotions, oils, sugar and salt scrubs and hair treatments.

- Instead of buying a whole bunch of cheap lipstick tubes, invest in two shades of lipstick from a quality company such as MAC.

- Learn how to look your most beautiful with the least amount of makeup or false hair.

- Try to find a less expensive gym membership. Or you can buy yoga, aerobic or pilates DVDs or VHS tapes and exercise at home.

Miscellaneous

- Use your fireplace for heat instead of turning the thermostat up higher.

- If possible consider sharing one car with your husband for the first year or two after your baby is born.

- Cut coupons and make sure that you have those club-saving cards for your local grocery store.

- Don't use a debit card, take cash out of the bank on a budgeted and weekly basis.

These are all just some suggestions on how to save money after the baby is born. If you and your husband are well off enough that you don't have to cut coupons then that's great. Many couples, however, do have to find a way to save money in order to give the best to a new and constantly growing baby.

In addition to cutting costs, you should think about saving for your children's college education. Also establish a trust fund and write a will for your estate that includes your children. It really is wise to do this even before your children are born. In essence you and your husband will be taking measures and steps that any other financially aware couple would make after having a baby.

❖AFRAID TO LET HALF-SIBLINGS NEAR YOUR BABY?

There is no denying that once you have a baby with your husband you will be very protective of that child, especially if you are a mother for the first time. This kind of cautious behavior comes with the territory of being a parent. But in addition to your normal concerns you may be hesitant to let your husband's children with BM near your baby. Believe it or not, this feeling of anxiety is normal.

If BM has programmed her children to disrespect you or even your husband, then how are you supposed to trust them to be gentle with your children? When I was pregnant I had horrible visions of my husband's children teasing my daughter, or trying to hit or hurt her when no one was looking. The surprisingly cruel things that BM had influenced them to say and do to me was proof enough of the potential my husband's children had to hurt my daughter. But I had to pull myself out of the victim mode and decide how I was going to handle the integration of my daughter and my husband's other two children. The fact was that although they may not have been raised with the same morals, spiritual beliefs or even manners, my husband was equally father to my daughter and to his other two children. I had to decide how I was going to make it a positive situation instead of one with a dark cloud over it.

Hopefully you are lucky enough to have stepchildren who are not cruel or disrespectful. If you've just given birth, you nor your husband deserve to have that kind of nasty energy in your home. That's why it's best to prepare your stepchildren for the birth of a new sibling before the baby is born. It may take them some time to get over mixed feelings and you and your husband want to help them move beyond this point. It may be especially hard if BM tells them things like, "Ya'll know your father's gonna treat that new baby better than you" or "That baby is not going to be related to you."

All of these aspects will mold the way that your stepchildren behave toward your children. After you've observed the temperament of your stepchildren, you and your husband can decide how you'd like to integrate them with your new baby.

If your stepchildren are:

Generally kind and respectful then you may try to arrange for them to see the baby in the hospital after you and your husband have bonded with your newborn. I suggest this only under the circumstance that you are certain BM will not try to storm into the maternity ward and start a commotion or ruin what should be a sacred set of memories for you and your family. After that or even before the baby's born you can teach your stepchildren how to help you take care of the baby. Tell your stepchildren how you expect them to treat your baby, their younger sibling. If your stepchildren are usually obedient then a new baby should be a rewarding chance to feel even more like a family. Try to get over whatever insignificant prejudices you might have toward your stepchildren and BM so that your husband can enjoy being with all of his children peacefully when he can. You'll be blessed for being so charitable and kind with your husband, your baby and your heart.

Moody and sometimes rude then you and your husband should try to help them accept that they will have a new half-sibling before the baby is born. This will give your husband some time to see where his children's state of mind really is. You and your husband should decide carefully if you want to bring his children near your newborn at the hospital. When you finally bring the baby home, it will take some time until you feel that you can trust your stepchildren to be alone with your baby. Don't feel pressured to do so. When your stepchildren earn your trust you will allow them sensible privileges with your baby. Your husband should try to arrange family counseling as it may help to make a good change in your stepchildren's behavior.

Definitely disrespectful, defiant and cruel then you and your husband should try to help them accept the idea of having a new sibling before you even get pregnant. The more time they have to accept the idea, the more time you have to turn their negative feelings into positive ones. Sorry, but if your stepchildren are highly unpleasant toward you then they should not be at the hospital after you give birth. That is too much of a risk to you and your baby. Chances are that if your stepchildren are so horrid, BM isn't much better. You don't want the possibility of either energy around you after you've given birth. This day belongs to you, your husband and your baby. Anyone else who wants to be a part of your circle should be worthy. When you bring your baby home do not ever leave your stepchildren alone with your child. As your child gets older use the same discretion. Your son or daughter may be faced with the possibility of mental, physical or yes, even sexual abuse at the hands of an older, jealous half-sibling. In some cases you may just have to keep your husband's older children away from your baby until a serious change in behavior takes place. It's not your job to worry about whether or not you appear to be a smug, new mother. It is your job to protect your child, no matter how old he or she is.

❖YOUR EXPECTATIONS FROM HIS FAMILY

You have seen how attached your husband's family is toward his children. In your heart you can only hope that his family will accept your precious children just as much. Every child deserves to be a part of their paternal and maternal grandparents', aunts', uncles' and cousins' lives. There is an emotional and social richness that extended family relationships provide for all of us. Yet still you wonder, *Will my husband's mother be excited to be a grandmother to our children, too? Is my husband's father going to welcome our new son or daughter into his life?*

Don't immediately imagine that just because your husband had other children before yours that his family will embrace them more than your child. Your husband's family has their own history with BM and they have formed an opinion of her, too. It's quite possible that their assessment of BM isn't as peachy as you think it is. His family is probably very happy and excited to have you join their circle. Why wouldn't they be equally excited to accept your beautiful babies?

Before you make any assumptions about how your husband's family will treat your children take a look at your own relationship with them. Are you friendly toward your husband's family members or do you treat them as if they have tuberculosis? Do you invite his sisters and brothers over for lunch and dinner? Do you call your mother-in-law just to say hello or do you wait until she calls you first? You have to make an effort to show his family that you are grateful to be married to your husband, who is their kin.

Don't go trying to get close with your husband's family members that are crazy, untrustworthy or reckless. Just make sure that those family members who are stable enough to be in your company know that they are always welcome. There are many ways to connect with extended family. Emails, snail mail, phone calls or even little greeting cards can really show someone that you've kept them in your mind.

After your baby is born be sure to send birth announcements to your husband's family. Maybe his family was very involved in your pregnancy from the very beginning. If so, good for you. If not, don't sweat it. Move past whatever feelings you may harbor about what appears to be their indifference to the joyous event in your life. Call them and share the good news with them. As your family grows, send them photographs of you, your husband and your children. You'd be surprised at how many of your husband's family members will respond positively.

Here are some tips on doing your part to facilitate a good relationship between your children and your husband's side of the family:

Grandparents: Don't forget to send pictures of your growing children to your husband's parents. Send a card on Grandparent's Day, Mother's and Father's Day and on their birthdays. You don't have to send a gift or card on each of these days, pick the ones that mean the most to you and your family. Allow your children to speak to their grandparents and to visit them often, if possible. Try sending home videos or tape-recorded messages, too. And until your baby can write, "I love you, Grandma/Grandpa" on a card, write it for her.

Aunts and Uncles: Get a list of their birthdays and send a birthday card with your children's pictures and hand-written letters. Find out what their favorite hobbies or talents are and let your children draw pictures or make gifts that are connected to their aunts' and uncles' interests.

Cousins: Most children enjoy having cousins as playmates. Try to arrange play dates with your children's paternal aunts and uncles so that your children can play together and experience the fun that comes with having cousins. Take pictures with your children and their cousins and give a framed copy to the cousin for a keepsake. If your children's cousins on your husband's side are old enough, have a sleepover with them AND your children's cousins from your side of the family.

Don't be stingy on holidays, either. Spend at least some part of Thanksgiving with your husband's side of the family if you can. The same goes for other holidays. In general remember the birthdays, hobbies and telephone numbers of your husband's family members. If you don't know this information for some of them, then ask around so that you can obtain it.

Your husband must do his part to maintain a good relationship with his family, but even if he hasn't then maybe you can be the bridge to repairing his strained relationship with some of his relatives. There's nothing odd about a wife reaching out to her husband's extended family. Chances are you'll receive more blessings and happy memories if you take a chance and show that you welcome them into your children's lives.

❖WHEN YOUR HUSBAND'S FAMILY IS UNFAIR

As for those of you who have tried all of these methods and found that your husband's family does indeed have some prejudice toward your child that is rooted in their feelings toward you, then don't break your neck trying to include them in your life. You are a wife and a mother. Your priority is making sure that your own immediate family is as snug as a bug in a rug.

You don't want to drain yourself trying to put a puzzle together that was already missing pieces before you came along. If his family behaves as if they don't want the privilege of being close to you, your husband or your children then **let it be**. You shouldn't try to force anyone to embrace you or your family. It is not a good example for your children.

One day your children will ask you why they are not close to their father's side of the family and you and your husband should find an honest and tactful way to explain this misfortune. Make sure that your children know that they are perfect and beautiful in every way and that it is not their fault that your husband's family members don't have any manners or finesse. If your husband's family ever does come around, then let your children bond with them comfortably at their own pace.

11

get ready to live a drama-free life

❖YOU'RE PREPARED

Now that you have given yourself a crash course on handling the Baby's Mama Monster there's only one thing left to do—and that is CELEBRATE!

Reading this book has certainly prepared you to tackle many of the common problems that women just like you have faced with a no-good BM. You are now better equipped to react in a manner that will benefit you in the long run. It will be easier to deal with stepchildren issues because hopefully I've helped you become a better stepmother, too. You have taken the time to understand how you can improve your situation instead of allowing someone else's inconsiderate behavior to control your atmosphere.

You've taken charge of how your husband's past will affect your future, so you no longer have a reason to sit around and complain to your girlfriends about how miserable BM is making you and your husband. Think about the times when you just reacted to BM or even your stepchildren out of your anger, pride or fear. It was draining, wasn't it? At the time you didn't have the tools to steer you into a more positive direction. Now you are clearly on your way to a more satisfying marriage and a calmer personal space.

Throughout your life you have probably taken many steps to build a wall of trust, safety and happiness around yourself and those you love. It isn't fair that your marriage to your husband should mean that your efforts are now meaningless. Your husband's connection to BM does not give her the right to ruin your hopes for a peaceful life. I commend you on being brave enough to uphold your social standards and your rights as a wife.

BM's rude behavior, her lies, threats of violence and whatever other shameless ploys she uses should no longer confuse you. From now on use your wisdom that you've gained as a guide in reacting to BM's behavior. Use your intelligence and your assertiveness to maintain your dignity when BM tries to drag your spirit down with hers. Revert to the lessons you've learned so that you don't have to waste your time making senseless mistakes.

You have so much more to do with your time now that you know how to handle BM. You have a husband who wants to make you happy despite the mess his BM has tried to take him through. You have stepchildren who need you to be an example of a kind and gentle person. At this point you need to find ways of rejuvenating yourself after such a trying journey. Don't stall here now that you've gained the power to see beyond BM's nonsense. Pat yourself on the back and move on to everything else that life has to offer.

❖YOU'RE CONFIDENT AND NOT AFRAID ANYMORE

So many wives are afraid to assert themselves when faced with Baby Mama Drama. They fear that they will make their husbands upset or incur BM's wrath. These wives fail to understand that by wallowing in fear, they're torturing themselves on BM's behalf. Who is BM to come into your life and make you afraid for standing up for yourself or your husband? You know now that as long as you have confidence in your right to exist on this planet everything else will fall into place.

If wives don't take an active role in creating a serene and safe marriage for themselves then what's the point in being married? You and your husband might as well choose the single life again if you allow someone to dictate the tone in your marriage. BM may always believe that she has the right to be difficult and rude, or even violent. You know now that your job is not to change BM's belief system, but to make sure that she doesn't smear her morals all over yours. Let BM continue to be who she is as long as you don't have to sacrifice the atmosphere that you and your husband need.

Doesn't it feel good to be back in charge? Doesn't it feel empowering to see BM for who she really is? Until BM grows up enough to begin acting with some sense and some self-respect, then chances are you haven't seen the last of her ignorance. Don't be afraid to express or protect yourself. There are many avenues that will ensure that you are protected from a melee with a rude, money-hungry, violent or crazy BM. As long as you and your husband pursue these avenues when the need arises you should put your fears and worries to rest.

In facing BM-related issues confidence and courage will steer you in the right direction. But confidence doesn't mean that you should become cocky or antagonistic in hopes of taunting BM. Remain the beautiful person you are and try your best not to start any static if you can avoid it. Everyone likes to tango with their inner machismo, but when it comes to BM she's far from a civil tango partner. Slam dancing is more her forte.

❖You're a Wonderful Wife and Stepmother

Despite everything BM has said and done to make you act out or sink to her level, you've remained on top. You have learned how to not blame your husband for her behavior and you haven't taken out your anger on your stepchildren. You have walked this tightrope without falling. It's time you stepped down and walked on sturdy ground.

It takes a smart and determined woman to constantly focus on the happiness of her marriage when she may be faced with prejudiced family members on her husband's side, possibly brainwashed stepchildren and an incurable BM. After dealing with all of that, who wants to muster up the energy to prepare a candlelit dinner for two? What wife will have the desire to spend quality time with her husband when the ugly subject of BM's behavior always comes up?

Many married couples can lose sight of their loving connection because of the negative energy that BM has tried to fuse into their circle. You and your husband should be proud that you overcame the obstacles that you have faced together. It doesn't mean that you're suckers for a hard life, it means that you want the best for yourselves and will go through the fire to come out, as Claude McKay wrote, stronger souls with finer frames.

Your stepchildren may not ever be blessed enough to know that you tried your best to keep their feelings and interest in mind. Maybe as they get older they will be able to understand. They don't know that you had to look deep within yourself to trust them, to forgive them for hurting your feelings at times and to objectively acknowledge their right to be a part of their father's life. After examining your situation and BM's influence on her children, you learned that BM is doing her children a great disservice and robbing them of their childhood experience.

It is no surprise that you have overcome the hurt of dealing with children who have been trained to disrespect you, even in your own home. How many times did you bite your tongue so that you wouldn't hurt your stepchild's feelings? In the end you have learned to empathize with innocent children who have been robbed of a peaceful and innocent relationship with their father and you, thanks to their egomaniacal mama. You and your husband, should you have your own children together, can really look forward to raising them without all of the ugliness that BM has forced upon your stepchildren. Through BM's ignorance you and your husband have probably created an even more sacred definition of parenthood.

❖YOU ARE KIND ENOUGH TO SHARE YOUR HUSBAND

It doesn't matter how many times BM has accused you of being the tyrannical force that robbed her children of a father. BM has yet to show your husband the respect that any good father deserves. She fails to acknowledge how gentle, thoughtful and protective he is of their children. Don't be amazed that BM refuses to admit that she is her worst enemy.

It may just irk BM that you are caring enough to remind your husband to call his children, to visit their teachers and to do loving extra things for them. It would be a lot easier if you really were the witch she professes you to be. But instead of living up to her expectations of being a cruel stepmother, you've gone over the river and through the woods to remain a shining example of a woman who isn't afraid to allow her husband to be the father he needs to be.

You have supported your husband in his quest to spend time with his children. You haven't discouraged him from pursuing a positive co-parenting relationship with BM. So why is it that BM still has a big issue with you? Why is it that BM still believes you put your husband under a spell that has made him shun her and their children? BM's emotional stability and outlook are skewed so no matter what you do, she will always want to paint an unfair picture of you to the world.

You and your husband know the deal. You know what efforts you made in order to keep the lines of communication open in what you hoped would be an amicable blended family. There's only so much you can do. After you've given your best on your stepchildren and your husband's behalf, BM must step up to the plate and make an effort, too. You have been kind enough to share your husband willingly. It's no secret that all wives are not like this. The amount of tenderness you've shown to your stepchildren may never be acknowledged by BM, so don't expect a thank-you note in the mail anytime soon. It is so very obvious that your stepchildren are lucky that their father married a woman like you.

❖YOU'RE BRIGHT AND PRODUCTIVE

I know you've felt like kicking BM's ass at times. You've pondered over the fairness of child support payments. You've felt like maybe even your marriage was a mistake. It's bugged out how we let outside harmful people or influences have such profound effects on us. It takes a while to master protecting your spirit from people like BM. Nevertheless, you've stayed productive and made sure that you continually evolved in all other areas of your life. At least I hope you have.

It can be very depressing to know that some ghetto, lying, vindictive person has access to your life, even if it's indirectly. Many wives become obsessed with how they can make BM disappear and as a result they ignore all other aspects of their own development. They forget about perfecting their talents. They no longer enjoy their hobbies. They become stagnant while they slip into BM's underworld.

One of the most rewarding things I did for myself while I was going through the drama, was to continually make room for my own evolution. I knew that BM would like nothing more than to see me fall into the Grand Canyon without a parachute. But did that stop me from taking trips into New York City for dance classes? Did I become a doleful, moping person at my place of employment? Did this stop me from learning more about different things that piqued my interest? No way! I paid attention to myself and made sure that I nurtured myself socially and intellectually. I was not going to turn into a purposeless woman at the hands of another one.

I made my situation the catalyst for new and exciting experiences. One of my hobbies is writing. I published personal essays and pieces of fiction. I even reached out and sought the career advice of other established writers in the newspaper and magazine industry. Instead of bashing BM's car windows out, I channeled my energy into actions that I knew would be cathartic for me. Most importantly, I began writing this book.

Please continue to enjoy your hobbies and explore self-development. Try cooking new recipes and surprise your husband every now and then. Enroll in a class that will enhance your career or your creative gifts. Redecorate your bedroom or bathroom. Your life shouldn't stop simply because BM wishes that it would. Instead your life should become even more exciting and successful. The best and only revenge you should want against BM is to live your best life.

❖GIRL, YOU EVEN MANAGE TO LOOK GOOD!

In the midst of all of the madness, you have learned to appreciate your own beauty. You have taken pride in how you look as well as how you feel. And for you, taking care of yourself isn't about competing with BM. It's about rewarding yourself with what you deserve. And what do you deserve?

You don't deserve to walk around looking haggard and faded. You don't deserve to become overweight because you've turned to food to relieve your BM-related stress. You don't deserve to let your nails become ragged and your hair dirty and unkempt because you've become overwhelmed with stepchildren who carry BM's funk into your home. You don't deserve to look like you swam up from the ruins of the Titanic.

If you haven't, I hope that you have made a pledge to yourself to polish, primp and pamper all that is you, whenever you can by any means necessary. Again, taking care of yourself has nothing to do with competing with BM's looks. For all I know, you may think the BM in your life could be a double for a cleft-lipped gorilla on a NOVA special. My point is that as a woman who has endured any kind of stressful situation, it is easy to morph into a dull and lifeless person. It is easy to forget that you have a beautiful smile, smooth skin and a brick house body.

Your husband may try to convince you that you are beautiful on the outside, but no amount of flattery will give you the lift you need to bounce back. You have to take the initiative to honor the physical beauty that you were blessed with; no one else can do this for you.

By maintaining yourself on the outside you will avoid the trap of low-self esteem that many women fall into. You don't want to begin comparing yourself to other women (including BM) and negating your physical attributes. If you do then soon you and others around you will begin to believe that you are unattractive on the outside *and* the inside.

Give yourself a good deep hair conditioning. Get a manicure or a foot massage. Join the local gym and treat yourself to aromatherapy in the steam room (trust me, it is divine!). When was the last time you turned on some sensual music and took a nice, hot bath? Skip making dinner sometimes and let your husband take over in the kitchen while you take an invigorating run at a nearby park or track.

It is important to look your best as often as you can. It shows that you have pride in yourself and it makes you feel better about interacting with people throughout the day. Being married should also be a motivating factor in maintaining your beauty. You wouldn't want your husband to let his handsome looks go down the drain, would you? No one wants a spouse that looks like a reject from Showtime at the Apollo or the Gong Show. I suggest you make sure that you don't fall into either category, married or not.

When's the last time you looked into the mirror and studied how beautiful you really are? Have you marveled at how despite the negativity that BM tried to bring into your life that you haven't received one wrinkle? If you haven't been taking care of yourself emotionally, spiritually and mentally then of course it will show on the outside. Do yourself a favor and tend to your needs so that when you look in the mirror you blush.

❖THE SKY'S THE LIMIT FOR YOU AND YOUR HUSBAND

Here's where I take a step back so that you can move forward with your husband. Take your place by his side as his wife and his friend. Take your place by your stepchildren's side as a trusted and fair adult who will always make an effort to welcome them into your life (even if they have been trained to resist your efforts). Get ready to continue your life as the happy, beautiful woman you once were before you were introduced to BM and her drama.

You married a man that you loved for his sensitivity, attractiveness, ambition and a host of other qualities, I'm sure. Despite what you may have heard your marriage to him doesn't mean that the ghosts of his past should be rattling chains in the attic. Not that you want to get rid of BM, you just don't want your life to be unnecessarily interrupted with her pettiness. BM needs to pick up her chains, and take her ghastly spirit out of your attic and at least attempt to create a life for herself. But since you've read this book, I guess you can call yourself an exorcist. From now on your attic should be pretty quiet.

The sky is the limit for you and your husband. You can have the family you want together. You can have the new house, the vacations, the peaceful family gatherings and the prank-free telephone calls. It takes time for you to eliminate a lot of the ugliness that may have crept into your life by way of BM, but with your husband's help it can be done.

The most important goal you should continue to have is to nurture your marriage. Your husband is your housemate, your friend, lover and teacher. It is the relationship with him that you must preserve. It doesn't matter if BM refuses to change, that's her burden to bear in life. You must change and grow and learn enough to enter a space in your marriage where BM's antics are powerless.

I can't believe I've come to the end of this book. I hope that it's been a worthwhile journey for you and I am honored that you trusted me as a traveling companion. Baby's Mama Drama may be a comical and well-intentioned humorous term, but for many women who have chosen to marry men with children from a previous relationship, it's not funny at all. Fortunately a crazy BM doesn't have to mean a life filled with embarrassing fiascos and restraining orders.

I wish you the best of luck as a stepmother, wife and most of all as an emotionally healthy and happy woman. Your husband must be very special if you have gone the extra mile to preserve your bond—I know my husband is worth the energy I put into writing this book. No amount of anybody's drama is powerful enough to take away the blessings that you and your husband are destined to share.

Here's to a drama-free and love-filled life. Cheers!

Appendix A

Child Support Glossary

Accrual

Sum of child support payments that are due or overdue.

Action Transmittal

Document sent out as needed, which instructs State child support programs on the actions they must take to comply with new and amended Federal laws. Has basis in Federal law and regulation.

Adjudication

The entry of a judgment, decree, or order by a judge or other decision-maker such as a master, referee, or hearing officer based on the evidence submitted by the parties.

Automated Administrative Enforcement of Interstate Cases (AEI)

Provision in the Personal Responsibility and Work Opportunity Reconciliation Act (PRWORA) giving States the ability to locate, place a lien on, and seize financial assets of delinquent obligors across State lines.

Administrative Procedure

Method by which support orders are made and enforced by an executive agency rather than by courts and judges.

Administration for Children and Families (ACF)

The agency in the Department of Health and Human Services (DHHS) that houses the Office of Child Support Enforcement (OCSE).

Affidavit

A written statement signed under oath or by affirmation, which is usually notarized.

Aid to Families with Dependent Children (AFDC)

Former entitlement program that made public assistance payments on behalf of children who did not have the financial support of one of their parents by reason of death, disability, or continued absence from the home; known in many States as ADC (Aid to Dependent Children). Replaced with Temporary Aid to Needy Families (TANF) under the Personal Responsibility and Work Opportunity Reconciliation Act (PRWORA).

Alleged Father

A person who has been named as the father of a child born out of wedlock, but who has not been legally determined to be the father; also referred to as putative father.

Arrearage

Past due, unpaid child support owed by the non-custodial parent. If the parent has arrearages, s/he is said to be "in arrears."

Burden of Proof

The duty of a party to produce the greater weight of evidence on a point at issue.

Case

A collection of people associated with a particular child support order, court hearing, and/or request for IV-D services. This typically includes a Custodial Party (CP), a dependent(s), and a Non-custodial Parent (NCP) and/or Putative Father (PF). Every child support case has a unique Case ID number and, in addition to names and identifying information about its members, includes information such as CP and NCP wage data, court order details, and NCP payment history.

Case Initiation

First step in the child support enforcement process.

Case Law

Law established by the history of judicial decisions in cases.

Case Member

Participant in child support case; a member can participate in more than one case.

Case ID

Unique identification number assigned to a case.

Cash Concentration and Disbursement "Plus" (CCD+)

Standardized format used for electronic funds transmission (EFT) of child support withholdings from an employee's wages.

Central Registry

A centralized unit, maintained by every State IV-D agency that is responsible for receiving, distributing, and responding to inquiries on interstate IV-D cases.

Centralized Collection Unit

A single, centralized site in each State IV-D agency to which employers can send child support payments they have collected for processing. This centralized payment-processing site is called the State Disbursement Unit (SDU) and is responsible for collecting, distributing, and disbursing child support payments.

Child Support

Financial support paid by a parent to help support a child or children of whom they do not have custody. Child support can be entered into voluntarily or ordered by a court or a properly empowered administrative agency, depending on each State's laws. Child support can involve cases where:

IV-D cases, where the custodial party (CP) is receiving child support services offered by State and local agencies; (such services include locating a non-custodial parent (NCP) or putative father (PF); establishing paternity; establishing, modifying, and enforcing child support orders; collecting distributing, and disbursing child support payments).

IV-A cases, where the CP is receiving public assistance benefits and the case is automatically referred to the State Child Support Enforcement CSE) Agency so the State can recoup the cost of the benefits from the non-custodial parent (NCP) or defray future costs.

IV-E cases, where the child(ren) is being raised not by one of their own parents but in the foster care system by a person, family, or institution and the case is also automatically referred to the CSE to recoup or defray the costs of foster care.

Non IV-D orders, where the case or legal order is privately entered into and the CSE is not providing locate, enforcement, or collection services (called); often entered into during divorce proceedings.

The support can come in different forms, including:

Medical support, where the child(ren) are provided with health coverage, through private insurance from the non-custodial parent (NCP) or public assistance that is reimbursed whole or in part by the NCP, or a combination thereof.

Monetary payments, in the form of a one-time payment, installments, or regular automatic withholdings from the NCP's income, or the offset of State and/or Federal tax refunds and/or administrative payments made to the NCP, such as Federal retirement benefits.

Child Support Enforcement (CSE) Agency

Agency that exists in every State that locates non-custodial parents (NCPs) or putative fathers (PF), establishes, enforces, and modifies child support, and collects and distributes child support money. Operated by State or local government according to the Child Support Enforcement Program guidelines as set forth in Title IV-D of the Social Security Act. Also known as a "IV-D Agency".

Child Support Enforcement Network (CSENet)

State-to-State telecommunications network, which transfers detailed information between States' automated child support enforcement systems.

Complainant

Person who seeks to initiate court proceedings against another person. In a civil case the complainant is the plaintiff; in a criminal case the complainant is the State.

Complaint

The formal written document filed in a court whereby the complainant sets forth the names of the parties, the allegations, and the request for relief sought. Sometimes called the initial pleading or petition.

Consent Agreement

Voluntary written admission of paternity or responsibility for child support.

Consumer Credit Agencies (CCA)

Private agencies that a State can use to locate obligors to establish and enforce child support.

Consumer Credit Protection Act (CCPA)

Federal law that limits the amount that may be withheld from earnings to satisfy child support obligations. States are allowed to set their own limits provided they do not exceed the Federal limits. Regardless of the number or withholding orders that have been served, the maximum that may be withheld for child support is:

> Without arrearage
> 50% with a second family
> 60% Single
>
> With Arrearage
> 55% with a second family and 12+ weeks in arrears
> 65% Single 12+ weeks in arrears

Court Order

A legally binding edict issued by a court of law. Issued by a magistrate, judge, or properly empowered administrative officer. A court order related to child support can dictate how often, how much, what kind of support a non-custodial parent is to pay, how long he or she is to pay it, and whether an employer must withhold support from their wages.

Custodial Party (CP)

The person who has primary care, custody, and control of the child(ren).

Custody

Legal custody is a determination by a court which establishes with whom a child will live. Physical custody describes with whom the child is living regardless of the legal custody status. Joint custody occurs when two persons where legal and/or physical custody of the child(ren). Split custody occurs when 2 or more children from the same person are in the legal custody of different people.

Custody Order

Legally binding determination that establishes with whom a child shall live. The meaning of different types of custody terms (e.g., Joint Custody, Shared Custody, Split Custody) vary from State to State.

Decree

The judicial decision of a litigated action, usually in "equitable" cases such as divorce (as opposed to cases in law in which judgments are entered).

Default

The failure of a defendant to file an answer or appear in a civil case within the prescribed time after having been properly served with a summons and complaint.

Default Judgment

A decision made by the court or administrative authority when the respondent fails to respond or appear.

Defendant

The person against whom a civil or criminal proceeding is begun.

Dependent

A child who is under the care of someone else. Most children who are eligible to receive child support must be a dependent. The child ceases to be a dependent when they reach the "age of emancipation" as determined by State law, but depending on the State's provisions, may remain eligible for child support for a period after they are emancipated.

Direct Income Withholding

A procedure, whereby an income withholding order can be sent directly to the non-custodial parent's (NCP's) employer in another State, without the need to use the IV-D Agency or court system in the NCP's State. This triggers withholding unless the NCP contests, and no pleadings or registration are required. The Act does not restrict who may send an income withholding notice across State lines. Although the sender will ordinarily be a child support Agency or the obligee, the obligor or any other person may supply an employer with an income withholding order.

Disbursement

The paying out of collected child support funds.

Disposable Income

The portion of an employee's earnings that remains after deductions required by law (e.g., taxes) and that is used to determine the amount of an employee's pay subject to a garnishment, attachment, or child support withholding order.

Disposition

The court's decision of what should be done about a dispute that has been brought to its attention. For instance, the disposition of the court may be that child support is ordered or an obligation is modified.

Docket

A formal brief record of proceedings in court; minutes entries in case files; the calendar of a court or administrative tribunal. Some courts refer to filing a paper with the court as docketing.

Enforcement

The application of remedies to obtain payment of a child or medical support obligation contained in a child and/or spousal support order. Examples of remedies includes garnishment of wages, seizure of assets, liens placed on assets, revocation of license (e.g., drivers, business, medical, etc.), denial of U.S. passports, etc.

Family Support Act

Law passed in 1988, with two major mandates: Immediate Wage Withholding, unless courts find that there is good cause not require such withholding, or there is a written agreement between both parties requiring an alternative arrangement; and Guidelines for Child Support Award Amounts, which requires States to use guidelines to determine the amount of support for each family, unless they are rebutted by a written finding that applying the guidelines would be inappropriate to the case.

Federal Tax Refund Offset Program

Program that collects past due child support amounts from non-custodial parents through the interception of their Federal income tax refund, or an administrative payment, such as Federal retirement benefits. This program also incorporates the Passport Denial Program, which denies U.S. passports at the time of application when the applicant's child support debts exceed $5,000. In the future, the program will expand to include the revocation and/or restriction of already issued passports. The cooperation of States in the submittal of cases for tax interception is mandatory, while submittal of cases for administrative interception is optional. The Federal Tax Refund Offset Program is operated in cooperation with the Internal Revenue Service, the U.S. Department of Treasury's Financial Management Service (FMS), the U.S. Department of State, and State Child Support Enforcement (CSE) Agencies.

Fraud

A deception deliberately practiced in order to secure unfair or unlawful gain.

Garnishee

The person upon whom a garnishment is served.

Garnishment

A legal proceeding under which part of a person's wages and/or assets is withheld for payment of a debt. This term is usually used to specify that an income or wage withholding is involuntary.

Genetic Testing

Analysis of inherited factors to determine legal fatherhood or paternity.

Guidelines

A standard method for setting child support obligations based on the income of the parent(s) and other factors determined by State law. The Family Support Act of 1988 requires States to use guidelines to determine the amount of support for each family, unless they are rebutted by a written finding that applying the guidelines would be inappropriate to the case.

Hearing

A proceeding in which a judge or hearing officer listens to testimony and argument and makes a decision based on the information presented and the law as it applies to the facts.

Immediate Wage Withholding

An automatic deduction from income that starts as soon as the agreement for support is established.

Imputed Income

Fringe benefits provided to employees that may be taxable but which cannot be counted as additional disposable income that is subject to child support obligations.

Income

As defined by the Personal Responsibility and Work Opportunity Reconciliation Act of 1996 (PRWORA), income is any periodic form of payment to an individual, regardless of source, including wages, salaries, commissions, bonuses, worker's compensation, disability, pension, or retirement program payments and interest. All income (except imputed income; see above) is subject to income withholding for child support, pursuant to a child support order, but is protected by Consumer Credit Protection Act limits, both State and federal.

Income Withholding

Procedure by which automatic deductions are made from wages or income, as defined in the Personal Responsibility and Work Opportunity Reconciliation Act (PRWORA), to pay a debt such as child support. Income withholding often is incorporated into the child support order and may be voluntary or involuntary. The provision dictates that an employer must withhold support from a non-custodial parent's wages and transfer that withholding to the appropriate agency (the Centralized Collection Unit or State Disbursement Unit). Sometimes referred to as wage withholding.

Information Memorandum (IM)

Document that provides State child support enforcement agencies with information on program practices that can be useful to program improvement.

Initiating Jurisdiction

The State or county court, or administrative agency, which sends a request for action to another jurisdiction in interstate child support cases. The requested action can include a request for wage withholding or for review and adjustment of existing child support obligations. In cases where a State is trying to establish an initial child support order on behalf of a resident custodial parent, and they do not have Long Arm Jurisdiction (i.e., they cannot legally claim personal jurisdiction over a person who is not a resident), they must file a Two-State action under the Uniform Interstate Family Support Act (UIFSA) guidelines.

Intercept

A method of securing child support by taking a portion of non-wage payments made to a non-custodial parent. Non-wage payments subject to interception include Federal tax refunds, State tax refunds, unemployment benefits, and disability benefits.

Interstate Cases

Cases in which the dependent child and non-custodial parent (NCP) live in different States, or where two or more States are involved in some case activity, such as enforcement.

Judgment

The official decision or finding of a judge or administrative agency hearing officer upon the respective rights and claims of the parties to an action; also known as a decree or order and may include the "findings of fact and conclusions of law."

Legal Father

A man who is recognized by law as the male parent of a child.

Lien

A claim upon property to prevent sale or transfer of that property until a debt is satisfied.

Litigation

A civil action in which a controversy is brought before the court.

Locate

Process by which a non-custodial parent (NCP) or putative father (PF) is found for the purpose of establishing paternity, establishing and/or enforcing a child support obligation, establishing custody and visitation rights, processing adoption or foster care cases, and investigating parental kidnapping.

Locate Information

Data used to locate a Putative Father (PF) or non-custodial parent (NCP). May include their Social Security Number (SSN), date of birth (DOB), residential address, and employer.

Medical Support

Form of child support where medical or dental insurance coverage is paid by the non-custodial parent (NCP). Depending on the court order, medical support can be an NCP's sole financial obligation, or it can be one of several obligations, with child and/or spousal support being the others.

Motion

An application to the court requesting an order or rule in favor of the party that is filing the motion. Motions are generally made in reference to a pending action and may address a matter in the court's discretion or concern a point of law.

Monthly Support Obligation (MSO)

The amount of money an obligor is required to pay per month.

New Hire (NH) Data

Data on a new employee that employers must submit within 20 days of hire to the State Directory of New Hires (SDNH) in the State in which they do business. Minimum information must include the employee's name, address, and Social Security Number (SSN), as well as the employer's name, address, and Federal Employer Identification Number (FEIN). Some States may require or request additional data. Multistate employers have the option of reporting all of their newly hired employees to only one State in which they do business. This data is then submitted to the National Directory of New Hires (NDNH), where it is compared against child support order information contained in the Federal Case Registry (FCR) for possible enforcement of child support obligations by wage garnishment. New hire data may also be used at the State level to find new hires that have been receiving unemployment insurance or other public benefits for which they may no longer be eligible, helping States to reduce waste and fraud. Federal Agencies report this data directly to the NDNH. Also known as (W4) data, after the form used to report the employees.

New Hire Reporting

Program that requires that all employers report newly hired employees to the State Directory of New Hires (SDNH) in their State. This data is then submitted to the National Directory of New Hires (NDNH), where it is compared against child support order information contained in the Federal Case Registry (FCR) for possible enforcement of child support obligations by wage garnishment. Some data is also made available to States to find new hires that have been receiving unemployment insurance or other public benefits for which they may no longer be eligible, helping States to reduce waste and fraud.

Non-custodial Parent (NCP)

The parent who does not have primary care, custody, or control of the child, and has an obligation to pay child support. Also referred to as the obligor.

Obligation

Amount of money to be paid as support by a non-custodial parent (NCP). Can take the form of financial support for the child, medical support, or spousal support. An obligation is a recurring, ongoing obligation, not a onetime debt such as an assessment.

Obligee

The person, State agency, or other institution to which a child support is owed (also referred to as custodial party when the money is owed to the person with primary custody of the child).

Obligor

The person who is obliged to pay child support (also referred to as the non-custodial parent or NCP).

Office of Child Support Enforcement (OCSE)

The Federal agency responsible for the administration of the child support program. Created by Title IV-D of the Social Security Act in 1975, OCSE is responsible for the development of child support policy; oversight, evaluation, and audits of State child support enforcement programs; and providing technical assistance and training to the State programs. OCSE operates the Federal Parent Locator Service, which includes the National Directory of New Hires (NDNH) and the Federal Case Registry (FCR). OCSE is part of the Administration for Children and Families (ACF), which is within the Department of Health and Human Services (DHHS).

Office of Personnel Management (OPM)

The Federal Government's "Human Resources Agency."

Offset

Amount of money intercepted from a parent's State or Federal income tax refund, or from an administrative payment such as Federal retirement benefits, in order to satisfy a child support debt.

Order

Direction of a magistrate, judge, or properly empowered administrative officer.

Order/Notice to Withhold Child Support

The form to be used by all States that standardizes the information used to request income withholding for child support. According to the Uniform Interstate Family Support Act (UIFSA), this form may be sent directly from the initiating State to a non-custodial parent's employer in another State.

Passport Denial Program

Program created by the Personal Responsibility and Work Opportunity Reconciliation Act (PRWORA) of 1996 that is operated under the auspices of the Federal Tax Refund Offset Program. Under the Passport Denial Program, obligors with child support arrearages of at least $5000 that are submitted to the to the Federal Office of Child Support Enforcement (OCSE) for Tax Refund Offset are forwarded to the U.S. Department of State, which "flags" the obligor's name and refuses to issue a passport in the event they apply for one. After the obligor makes arrangements to satisfy the arrears, States can decertify them with OCSE, which then requests that the State Department remove them from the program. This program is automatic, meaning that any obligor that is eligible will be submitted to the State Department unless the State submitting the case for Tax Offset specifically excludes them from the Passport Denial Program.

Paternity

Legal determination of fatherhood. Paternity must be established before child or medical support can be ordered.

Payee

Person or organization in whose name child support money is paid.

Payor

Person who makes a payment, usually non-custodial parents or someone acting on their behalf, or a custodial party who is repaying a receivable.

Plaintiff

A person who brings an action; the party who complains or sues in a civil case.

Pleadings

Statements or allegations, presented in logical and legal form, which constitute a plaintiff's cause of action or a defendant's grounds of defense.

Policy Interpretation Question (PIQ)

An official reply by the Federal Office of Child Support Enforcement (OCSE) to an inquiry submitted by a State child support agency concerning application of policy. Although questions often arise from a specific practice or situation, the responses are official statements of OCSE policy on the issue.

Putative Father (PF)

The person alleged to be the father of the child but who has not yet been medically or legally declared to be the Legal Father.

Referral

Request sent to a IV-D agency from a non IV-D agent or agency asking that a child support case be established.

Respondent

The party answering a petition or motion.

Review and Adjustment

Process in which current financial information is obtained from both parties in a child support case and evaluated to decide if a support order needs to be adjusted.

Spousal Support

Court ordered support of a spouse or ex-spouse; also referred to as maintenance or alimony.

State Case Registry (SCR)

A database maintained by each State that contains information on individuals in all IV-D cases and all non IV-D orders established or modified after October 1, 1998. Among the data included in the SCR is the State's numerical FIPS code, the State's identification number (which must be unique to the case), the case type (IV-D vs. Non IV-D), locate information on persons listed in the case, in addition to other information. Information submitted to the SCR is transmitted to the Federal Case Registry, where it is compared to cases submitted to the FCR by other States, as well as the employment data in the National Directory of New Hires (NDNH). Any matches found are returned to the appropriate States for processing.

State Directory of New Hires

A database maintained by each State, which contains information regarding newly hired employees for the respective State. The data is then transmitted to the NDNH, where it is compared to the employment data from other States as well as child support data in the Federal Case Registry (FCR). Any matches found are returned to the appropriate States for processing. Employers are required to submit new hire data to the SDNH within 20 days of the hire date. Multistate employers (those that do business and hire workers in more than one State) have additional options on where to report new hire information. In most States, the SDNH is contained in the State Parent Locator Service (SPLS) that is part of each State IV-D agency, in others it is operated by the State Employment Security Agency (SESA).

Support Order

A judgment, decree, or order, whether temporary, final, or subject to modification, issued by a court or an administrative agency of a competent jurisdiction, for the support and maintenance of a child. This includes a child who has attained the age of majority under the law of the issuing State, or of the parent with whom the child is living. Support orders can incorporate the provision of monetary support, health care, payment of arrearages, or reimbursement of costs and fees, interest and penalties, and other forms of relief.

Subpoena

A process issued by a court compelling a witness to appear at a judicial proceeding. Sometimes the process will also direct the witness to bring documentary evidence to the court.

Summons

A notice to a defendant that an action against him or her has been commenced in the court issuing the summons and that a judgment will be taken against him or her if the complaint is not answered within a certain time.

Tribunal

The court, administrative agency, or quasi-judicial agency authorized to establish or modify support orders or to determine parentage.

Two-State Action

Action a State must file under the Uniform Interstate Family Support Act (UIFSA) guidelines when it does not have Long Arm Jurisdiction (i.e., cannot legally claim personal jurisdiction over a non-custodial parent who lives in another State). This is usually in cases where a State is trying to establish an initial child support order on behalf of a resident custodial party. Other actions, such as requesting wage withholding or reviewing and/or revising an existing support order, do not require a Two-State Action even if the initiating State does not have Long Arm Jurisdiction.

Wage Assignment

A voluntary agreement by an employee to transfer (or assign) portions of future wage payments (e.g., insurance premium deductions, credit union deductions) to pay certain debts, such as child support.

Wage Attachment

An involuntary transfer of a portion of an employee's wage payment to satisfy a debt. In some States this term is used interchangeably with Wage or Income

Withholding, in other States there are distinctions between an attachment and withholding. The most common term used is Wage or Income Withholding.

Wage Withholding

A procedure by which scheduled deductions are automatically made from wages or income to pay a debt, such as child support. Wage withholding often is incorporated into the child support order and may be voluntary or involuntary. The provision dictates that an employer must withhold support from a non-custodial parent's wages and transfer that withholding to the appropriate agency (the Centralized Collection Unit or State Disbursement Unit). Also known as income withholding.

APPENDIX B

Recommended Resources

Web sites

These are great Web sites that offer information for stepmothers, new wives and parents in general. Don't be afraid to participate in the forums or message boards. You'd be surprised at how much insight you can gain from or give to the women on the board.

Smart Marriages
www.smartmarriages.com

Blended Families Resource Guide
www.blendedfamily.com

A Stepmom's Haven
http://communities.msn.com/AStepmomsHaven

CoMamas Association
www.comamas.com

StepCarefully for Stepparents
www.stepcarefully.com

Successful Stepfamilies
www.successfulstepfamilies.com

Parentline Plus
www.parentlineplus.org.uk

IVillage
www.ivillage.com
www.ivillage.com/relationships

Parent Soup
www.parentsoup.com

books & other reads

Here are some books that might give you and your husband a helping hand in dealing with Baby Mama Drama. Some of these books are written specifically for stepfamilies, and others are books with great wisdom on facing adversity and enjoying your life as it should be.

Your Stepfamily Magazine
www.yourstepfamily.com

Family Digest Magazine
www.familydigest.com

Keys to Successful Stepmothering
By Philippa Greene Mulford

Stepmotherhood: How to Survive Without Feeling Frustrated, Left Out, or Wicked
By Cherie Burns

Stepcoupling: Creating and Sustaining a Strong Marriage in Today's Blended Family
By Susan Wisdom and Jennifer Green

What Black Men Should Do Now: 100 Simple Truths, Ideas, and Concepts
K. Thomas Oglesby, Tavis Smiley

Blessed Health: The African-American Woman's Guide to Physical and Spiritual Well-Being
By Melody T. McCloud and Angela Ebron

Power of Being a Real Woman
By Jennifer Keitt

Warrior Lessons: An Asian American Woman's Journey Into Power
By Phoebe Eng

Sacred Pampering Principles: An African-American Woman's Guide to Self-Care and Inner Renewal
By Debrena Jackson Gandy

Husband's Little Black Book: Common Sense, Wit and Wisdom for a Better Marriage
By Robert J. Ackerman

organizations

Here are some organizations that you may want to contact for more information on living in a blended family.

The Stepfamily Association of America
650 J Street, Suite 205
Lincoln, NE 68508
1-800-735-0329/fax 1-477-8317
www.saafamilies.org

The Stepfamily Network
555 Bryant Street, #361
Palo Alto, CA 94301
Tel: (800) 487-1073
www.stepfamily.net

Alliance for Marriage
P.O. Box 2490
Merrifield, VA 22116
www.allianceformarriage.org

bibliography

American Psychiatric Association: *Diagnostic and Statistical Manual of Mental Disorders*, Fourth Edition, Text Revision. (Washington. DC: American Psychiatric Association, 2000).

Doherty, Ph.D, William, J. "Finding a Good Therapist."
http://westhartfordcounselingcenter.com/findone.htm

Drucker, David H. "What is Parental Alienation Syndrome?"
www.suite101.com/article.cfm/14651/69627

Lofas, Jeannette, CSW. *Stepparenting* (New York: Kensington Books 1996).

Love, Patricia. *Emotional Incest Syndrome: What to Do When a Parent's Love Rules Your Life.* (New York: Bantam Books, 1991).

National Office of Child Support Enforcement. "Glossary of Child Support Enforcement Terms."
http://ocse.acf.hhs.gov/necsrspub/glossary.cfm

Thompson, Colleen M.S. R.D. "Finding a Therapist."
http://www.mirror-mirror.org/findther.htm

_____."Types of Mental Illnesses and Treatments"
http://www.rethink.org/information/med/

_____. "Understanding Mental Illness"
http://hcpc.uth.tmc.edu/mentalillnesses.htm

_____. National Alliance for Mental Illnesses. "Information on Illnesses and Treatments."
http://web.nami.org/illness/

about the author

Ayesha J. Gallion, a former reporter for *The West Orange Chronicle*, received her B.A. in English with a concentration in journalism from Morgan State University in Baltimore, Maryland.

Ms. Gallion has been a high school English teacher for the Newark, New Jersey school system. She has also been an academic lesson planner for Americorps and the Baltimore Police Athletic League. Her writing has been published in *The Baltimore City Paper, Go Newark's* e-zine, *The East Orange Record, The News Record of Maplewood and South Orange* and the anthology *Role Call.* Before taking on this project Ms. Gallion was the associate news producer for *The Star-Ledger's* online affiliate NJ.com. She lives in East Orange with her husband and their daughter.

For all inquiries or comments relative to *No More Baby's Mama Drama* or Ms.Gallion correspondence should be sent to:

Ayesha J. Gallion
P.O. Box 3231
East Orange, NJ 07019

0-595-30305-6